Helion & Company Limited
Unit 8 Amherst Business Centre
Budbrooke Road
Warwick
CV34 5WE
England
Tel. 01926 499 619
Fax 0121 711 4075
Email: info@helion.co.uk
Website: www.helion.co.uk
Twitter: @helionbooks
Visit our blog http://blog.helion.co.uk/

Published by Helion & Company 2019
Designed and typeset by Farr out Publications, Wokingham, Berkshire
Cover designed by Paul Hewitt, Battlefield Design (www.battlefield-design.co.uk)
Printed by Henry Ling Limited, Dorchester, Dorset

Text © David Francois 2019
Illustrations © as individually credited
Aviation colour profiles and map drawn by and © Tom Cooper 2019, vehicle colour profiles drawn by and © David Bocquelet 2019

Every reasonable effort has been made to trace copyright holders and to obtain their permission for the use of copyright material. The author and publisher apologize for any errors or omissions in this work, and would be grateful if notified of any corrections that should be incorporated in future reprints or editions of this book.

ISBN 978-1-911628-68-2

British Library Cataloguing-in-Publication Data
A catalogue record for this book is available from the British Library

All rights reserved. No part of this publication may be reproduced, stored in a retrieval system, or transmitted, in any form, or by any means, electronic, mechanical, photocopying, recording or otherwise, without the express written consent of Helion & Company Limited.

We always welcome receiving book proposals from prospective authors.

CONTENTS

Abbreviations		2
Addenda/Errata to *Latin America@War 9: Nicaragua 1961-1990, the Downfall of the Somoza Dictatorship*		2
Introduction		4
1	The Nicaraguan Sandinistas	6
2	The Sandinista Forces	10
3	The Birth of the Contras (1980-1982)	21
4	The Undeclared War of the Reagan Administration (1981-1982)	27
5	Grenada 1983 – Nicaragua 1984	34
6	The Sandinista Counter-Offensive (1985-1986)	41
7	Between War and Peace (1986-1988)	50
8	The Long Road to Peace (1988-1990)	61
Selected Bibliography		66
Notes		67
Acknowledgements		72
Author		72

ABBREVIATIONS

ACE	Amalgamated Commercial Enterprises	JGRN	*Junta de Gobierno de Reconstrucción Nacional* (Junta of National Reconstruction)
AMNLAE	*Asociación de Mujeres Nicaragüenes Luisa Amanda Espinoza* (Luisa Amanda Espinoza Association of Nicaraguan Women)	KISAN	*Kus Indian Sut Asla Nicaragua ra* (Nicaraguan Coast Indian Unity)
APP	*Area de Propriedad del Pueblo* (People's Property Area)	Km	kilometre
		NCO	non-commissioned officer
ARDE	*Alianza Revolucionaria Democratica* (Democratic Revolutionary Alliance)	MDN	*Movimiento Democrático Nicaragüense* (Nicaraguan Democratic Movement)
ARDEN	*Alianza Democrática Revolucionaria Nicaragüense* (Nicaraguan Democratic Revolutionary Alliance)	MINDIRA	*Ministerio de Desarrollo y Instituto Nacional de Reforma Agraria*
		MINT	*Ministerio del Interio* (Interior ministry)
BLC	*Batallones de Lucha Cazador* (*Bataillon de chasseurs légers*)	MILPAS	*Milicias Populares Anti-Sandinistas* (Anti-Sandinista Popular Militias)
BLI	*Batallones de Lucha Irregular* (Light Battalion)	MPS	*Milicia Popular Sandinista* (Sandinista popular militia)
BOS	*Bloque Opositor del Sur* (Southern Opposition Bloc)	MISURA	Miskito, Sumo, and Rama
CDS	*Comités de Defensa Sandinista*	MISURATA	Miskito, Sumo, Rama Unity
CIA	Central Intelligence Agency (United States)	MISURASATA	Miskito, Sumo, Rama, and Sandinista Unity
COIN	counter-insurgent or counter-insurgency	NSC	National Security Council
CONDECA	*Consejo de Defensa Centroamericana* (Central American Defense Council)	OAS	Organization of American States
Col	colonel (military commissioned officer rank)	RN	*Resistencia Nicaragüense* (National Resistance)
COSEP	*Consejo Superior de la Empresa Privada* (Higher Council of Private Enterprises)	RM	*Region Militar* (Military Region)
		RPG	Rocket-propelled grenade
ENABAS	*Empresa Nicaragüense de Alimentos Básicos* (National Enterprise for Basic Foodstuffs)	SMP	*Servicio Militar Patriótico* (Patriotic Military Service)
EPS	*Ejercito popular sandinista* (Sandinista Popular Army)	UDN-FARN	*Union Democratica Revolucionaria Nicaraguense-Fuerzas Armadas Revolucionarias de Nicaragua* (Nicaraguan Democratic Union-Nicaraguan Revolutionary Armed Forces)
FAL	*Fusil Automatique Léger* (light automatic rifle, Belgian-designed firearm)	UN	United Nations
FDN	*Fuerza Democrática Nicaragüense* (Nicaraguan Democratic Force)	UNO	*Unión Nacional Opositora* (National Opposition Union)
FAS-DAA	*Fuerza Aérea sandinista y Defensa Antiaérea* (Sandinista Air Force-Air Force Defence)	UNO	*Unidad Nicaragüense Opositora* (United Nicaraguan Opposition)
FDN	*Fuerza Democratica Nicaragüense* (Nicaragua Democratic Force)	US	United States of America
		USMC	United States Marine Corps
FSLN	*Frente Sandinista de Liberación Nacional* (Sandinista National Liberation Front)	US$	United States Dollar
		USSR	Union of Soviet Socialist Republics (Soviet Union)
GDR	German Democratic Republic (East Germany)	YATAMA	*Yapti Tasba Masraka Nanih Aslatakanka* (Sons of Mother Earth)
Gen	general (military commissioned officer rank)		
GN	*Guardia Nacional* (National Guard)		
HQ	headquarters		

ADDENDA/ERRATA TO *LATIN AMERICA@WAR 9: NICARAGUA 1961-1990, THE DOWNFALL OF THE SOMOZA DICTATORSHIP*

Contemporary military history is a highly dynamic discipline, in which the research never ends, and new information is obtained almost continuously. Kike Maracas, a son of a former soldier of the National Guard of Nicaragua (GN), forwarded us the following commentary, updates and photographs in response to the publishication of Volume 1:

Page 15: Regarding the clash at 'Las Termópilas', in Managua, on 6 August 1967: the Sandinistas claimed that 300 soldiers attacked a cell of about four or five insurgents. Actually, it was a police unit that tried to enter the house first. The Sandinistas opened fire, killing one. The National Guard deployed a company of about 100, supported by one T17E1 Staghound armoured car. By the time the GN arrived on the scene, only one militant was still around. The commander of the National Guard then ordered the crew of the armoured car to open fire: that ended the confrontation.

Insignia of the BCS. (Kike Maracas)

Page 18: The 'Presidential Guard Battalion' was actually named the General Somoza Battalion, or BCS. It was a combat unit, not a 'personal guard' or a ceremonial unit. After the earthquake of 1972, it existed on paper only. It was re-established in 1978, staffed by a new complement of officers and other ranks – mostly graduates of the Infantry Training School (EEBI) – and deployed in combat. According to its commander, Colonel (Infantry) Alberto Smith, it had about 500 troops in total.

The GN remained a small outfit through 1978 and 1979: it never included more than between 5,500 and 6,500, including administrative personnel. Only about 2,000 were members of combat units. It never used M60 machine guns but Browning BAR, M1919 and the newer FN MAG58. The GN troops originally wore US-made M1 helmets. By 1978, these were replaced by Israeli-made OR-201 kevlar helmets. Some Galil assault rifles were in service by then. Uniforms were of Nicaraguan origin. Furthermore, the GN received a mix of FN FAL, M16A1s, and SAR assault rifles by 1979. Even then, between 30-40% of its troops were still armed with the very good M1 Garand rifle.

Regarding Staghounds: Israel offered a total of 90 Chevrolet M6/T17E1 and T17E2 armoured cars, in the late 1950s. After three months of testing, only the 80 best were chosen: 30 were sold to Cuba (then still under Bautista), 10 were held as reserve, and 40 pressed into active service with the Armoured Battalion of the GN. About 30 were still in service by 1977. Between eight and ten were knocked out during the final phase of the war in 1979, together with two Sherman tanks and two or three M3 halftracks, mostly in urban battles. The new Sandinista army originally operated 14 Staghounds, three Sherman tanks, four M3 halftracks and one 'do-it-yourself' armoured vehicle left behind by the BN.

At an unknown date in 1979, Emilio Miranga Mongalo, one of the Sandinista pilots involved in operations to deliver weapons and supplies to the insurgents inside Nicaragua, had an encounter with one of the Fuerza Aera (de) Nicaragua's Lockheed AT-33A Shooting Stars. The jet (serial number 306) attacked Miranga Mongalo's Cessna FTB.337 using machine guns. Realizing he could not escape, the Sandinista pilot made a belly landing in an open field, and escaped to Costa Rica on foot. As far as is known, this is what can be considered the only aerial victory of the Nicaraguan War of the 1960-1979 period.

Troops of the General Somoza Battalion, with one of their Dodge M37B jeeps, as seen in 1979. The unit also operated Ebro jeeps from Spain, Ford M151s, Unimog 404s and AIL M325 command cars. All troops used Israeli-made equipment and armament. (via Kike Maracas)

The GN also had commandos. They wore black berets and were considered special forces. This photograph shows them at a firing range in 1978, armed with SAR and Galil assault rifles, and wearing Israeli combat vests. Visible are vehicles including AIL M325 command cars, Dodge M37Bs and Pegaso 3050s. (Nicaraguan National Guard, via Kike Maracas)

Two M4 Sherman tanks of the First Armoured Battalion as seen on the southern front in June 1979, together with several T17E1 Staghounds. The prefix 'PBB' in their hull numbers stood for *Primer Batallón Blindado* ('First Armoured Battalion'). (Chaleco, via Kike Maracas)

This M3 halftrack of the GN was photographed in Esteli in 1978. Notable is additional armour plating atop the combat compartment. (Novedades via Kike Maracas)

INTRODUCTION

The Sandinista National Liberation Front's (FSLN) long struggle against the Somoza regime has long received no international attention. It was not until 1978 that events in Nicaragua made the headlines. The civil war that began after the Sandinistas came to power, like the Vietnam War, quickly polarized world opinion, since like the latter the conflict in Nicaragua became a new emblematic front in the dynamics of the East-West confrontation.

The arrival of the Sandinista regime, which, according to many observers, transformed Nicaragua into a "second Cuba", took place at a time when the USSR seemed to be leading a global offensive; Soviets and Cubans played an active role in Angola in 1975-1976, Ethiopia in 1977-1978, in the overthrow of the Cambodian Khmer Rouge by Vietnam in 1978, and Moscow intervened in Afghanistan in December 1979, only a few months after the fall of Somoza. On the Western side,

Troops of the GN undergoing training at the Infantry School in 1978. (via Kike Maracas) Caption:

Troops of the 3rd Company GN, with Israeli-made OR-201 kevlar helmets and combat vests. (AP, via Kike Maracas

the disastrous evacuation of Saigon in 1975 and the US humiliation in Tehran in 1980 encouraged the arrival in power of supporters of firmness in international politics with the election of Ronald Reagan as President of the United States. Under these conditions, the struggle against revolutionary Nicaragua became a major objective for the new administration and a symbol of its desire to push back communism in the world.

While the conflict in Nicaragua was part of the world-wide conflict, it also had internal origins and reflected the deep divisions in Nicaraguan society in the face of the upheavals brought about by the Sandinista revolutionary project. It was therefore taking place at different levels, at the crossroads of the great powers' ambitions, the regional balances in Central America and the tensions that agitated Nicaragua. It embodied especially the hopes and fears generated by the last revolutionary experience of the 20th century.

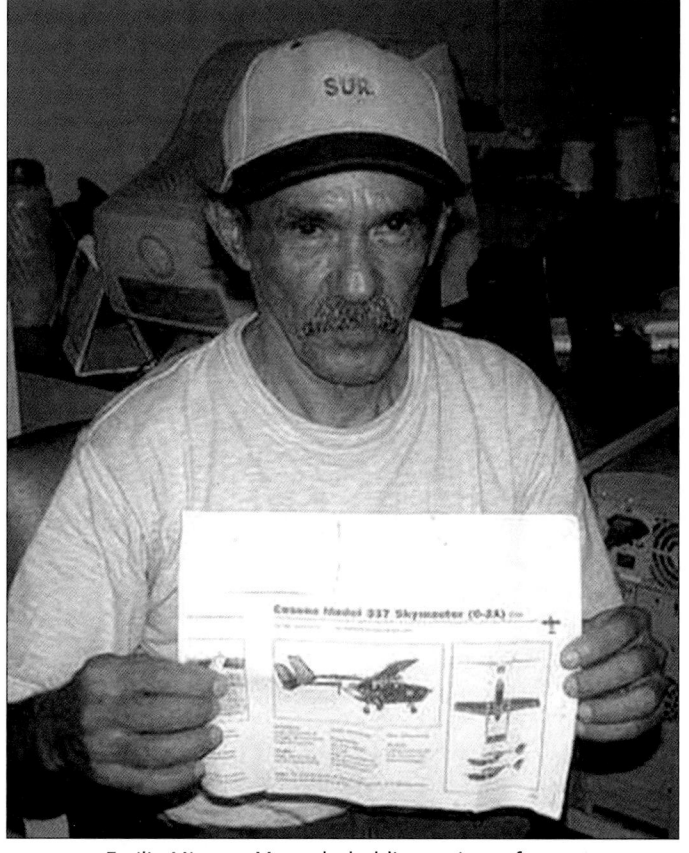

Emilio Miranga Mongalo, holding a piece of paper with the type of aircraft he flew when intercepted by a FAN AT-33A. (Courtesy *El Nuevo Diario*)

1

THE NICARAGUAN SANDINISTAS

On 17 July 1979, Anastasio Somoza Debayle left Nicaragua and 33 years of dictatorship ended. Two days later, the victorious troops of all FSLN guerrilla Fronts made a triumphal entry into the capital, Managua. The months following the overthrow of the dictatorship were marked by a strong popular enthusiasm and incredible optimism. Delinquency disappeared and it was teenagers of the popular militias who maintained public order while popular festivals were organized in the neighbourhoods.[1]

The enthusiasm that accompanied the first steps of the new power could not hide the ruin that overwhelmed the country. GDP fell by 26.4% in 1979, external debt stood at $1.6 trillion, agricultural exports were at their lowest, inflation was 60%, and severe shortages occurred. But in July 1979, joy and hope were without measure. Nicaragua, the rest of Central America, and the democratic world celebrated the triumph of a people against the abuses of the tyrant. The revolution was realized on principles and objectives shared by all the actors of the coalition against Somoza and defined by the agreement of Puntarenas: political pluralism, the establishment of a mixed economy and a foreign policy based on non-alignment. But soon, the victors of July were divided on each of these issues to the point of tipping Nicaragua into a new civil war.

The Sandinisation of Power

The anti-Somozoist alliance which settled in Managua promulgated on 20 July the Fundamental Statutes of the Republic of Nicaragua which laid the foundations of a provisional institutional order. The new power was based on the *Junta de Gobierno de Reconstrucion Nacional* (JGRN), formed of 5 members in Costa Rica even before the fall of Somoza. The FSLN was theoretically a minority in the JGRN since it was represented only by Daniel Ortega Saavedra but two other members were sympathizers; Moisés Hassán Morales and the writer Sergio Ramírez Mercado, member of the FSLN since 1975. Violeta Barrios Chamorro and Alfonso Robelo Callejas, leader and founder of the Nicaraguan Democratic Movement (MDN) were in the minority.[2] And indeed those who led the actions of the Junta were Daniel Ortega and Sergio Ramirez.

The FSLN had significant popular support and Nicaraguans believed that the *Comandantes* would build a new and better society. The new power seemed to respond to these aspirations by launching the National Literacy Crusade between March and August 1980 when thousands of young people organized into brigades, taught about 500,000 peasants and reduced the illiteracy rate from 52% to 12%. In 1983, thousands of young people embarked on a new campaign on the health front, this time to fight against dengue and malaria.[3]

While waiting for election, the anti-Somoza coalition decided to establish a Council of State that would act as a sort of parliament. It was decided that in this Council of State of 33 members, 11 would be designated by the FSLN which would therefore be in a minority. When the Council was set up in May 1980, the FSLN nevertheless decided that the number of seats would no longer be 33, but 47. Above all, it managed to appoint representatives of many organizations close to it, such as the Confederation Sandinista of Workers (CST), the National Union of Farmers and Breeders (UBAF), the Association of Nicaraguan Women Luisa Amanda Espinoza (AMNLAE) or the *Comités de Defensa Sandinista* (CDS). In this way,

A group of Sandinista combatants in 1979. The man in the centre is equipped with an RPG-2. (via Kike Maracas)

A group of FSLN guerrillas, as seen in 1978. Notable is their main armament consisting of FN FAL assault rifles. (Albert Grandolini Collection)

the Sandinistas obtained an absolute majority.[4] The next elections being planned to take place in five years, the non-Sandinista forces were effectively excluded from power for years.

The nine commanders of the revolution who formed the FSLN National Directorate quickly seized most of the key posts in the state apparatus. Daniel Ortega was president of the Junta before becoming President of the Republic. The economy was in the hands of Henry Ruiz, Minister of Planning, and Jaime Wheelock, Minister of Agriculture, who controlled agrarian reform. The security forces were led by Tomás Borge and Luis Carrión, Minister and Deputy Minister of the Interior. Bayardo Arce and Victor Tirado held the party apparatus and controlled Sandinista organizations.[5] In the Armed Forces, the Minister of Defence was at first non-Sandinista Bernardino Larios but from September 1979 his power was removed and he was sent back in December to be replaced by the leader of the Sandinista People's Army (*Ejercito popular sandinista* or EPS), Humberto Ortega. This process of taking control extended to all spheres of the state and was repeated in many institutions until 1982.

Within civil society, the FSLN controlled many mass organizations that supervised the population, such as the *Central Sandinista de Trabajadores* (Sandinista Workers' Centre or CST) among the workers, the UBAF among the small and medium farmers, the *Asociación de Trabajadores del Campo* (Rural Worker Association or ATC) among the landless peasants, and the AMNLAE among the women. Urban neighbourhoods were crisscrossed by CDSs, which played an important role in supplying, rationing and controlling the population. The few non-Sandinista social organizations were thus marginalized.

For the Sandinistas, sovereignty resided in the people of whom the FSLN, as avant-garde, was the expression. This postulate justified the Sandinista grip on all the wheels of society, politics and the economy of the country. It is for this reason that the FSLN National Directorate

The final drive of the FSLN was supported by several groups of 'foreign volunteers'- i.e. Cuban instructors: this photograph was taken while they were moving their recoilless rifles into position on the outskirts of Managua. (Albert Grandolini Collection)

Humberto Ortega, Luis Carrion, and Daniel Ortega shortly after taking over in Managua of 1979. (Photo by Pedro Meyer)

was also the real government of Nicaragua since it controlled the main state institutions: the JGRN, State Council and the main ministries.[6] It had thus gradually imposed a structure of power with strict control over the decision-making process, highly centralized and very vertical, accumulating a quasi-absolute power embodied by the Ortega brothers, one at the head of the administration and the political apparatus, the other to the leadership of the military force.

Nevertheless, the FSLN wanted to make a place for the "bourgeois" opposition. It left them positions in the JGRN, government and administrations. For a time this so-called pluralistic distribution was, on the one hand, respected by the FSLN and, on the other hand, accepted by the other political forces even if non-Sandinistas occupied only secondary positions in the administration.

On 19 April 1980, when Violeta Chamorro and Alfonso Robelo resigned from the JGRN to protest against the FSLN's hold on power, doubts ensued. From this moment, many non-Sandinistas resigned or went into exile in Costa Rica, Honduras or Miami. For example, the popular Eden Pastora was Deputy Minister of the Interior but had no power before resigning in July 1981 and joining the opposition in April 1982.

In a few years, all political power was in the Sandinistas' hands. This power was coupled with close control over civil society and the media. If the non-Sandinistas were marginalized, it was an area where the FSLN left them a large place, the economy.

The FSLN's Economic Policy

In the summer of 1979, the main economic ministries, with the exception of the agrarian reform, were entrusted to representatives of the private sector. It was for the FSLN to give a democratic image of openness especially to the nations of Western Europe and, more particularly, to those who were ready to provide assistance to Nicaragua. These ministers were succeeding in renegotiating the foreign debt and in coordinating the foreign aid received by the International Fund for Reconstruction. In the beginning, progress was made easily, foreign loans were important and the debt schedule was readjusted in two stages with generous conditions. Particular attention was given to the recovery of agricultural exports, wage increases remained below inflation rates, real GDP increased by 11% in 1980 and by 5.3% in 1981 while unemployment decreased from 28% in 1979 to 17% in 1980.[7]

The Sandinistas supported this moderate economic policy and when extreme left wing movements protested against what they saw as a betrayal of the revolution by organizing strikes and demonstrations, the FSLN reacted. It banned leftist groups in early 1980, but not to cut itself off from its grassroots base, it nonetheless accepted land occupations and accelerated the agrarian reform program in 1981. Economically, the FSLN and the private sector shared the same views, even if the Sandinistas wanted to establish socialism in Nicaragua, but this goal was planned in the long term.

While the private sector was essential for rebuilding the economy, the Sandinistas nonetheless strived to establish a mixed economy. In this perspective, the FSLN did not seek to suppress private ownership of the means of production but rather to regulate prices and wages to prevent abuse to the detriment of the poor. One of the first economic measures taken by the JGRN was the confiscation of land and property belonging to the Somoza family and relatives of the former regime which represented 1/5th of the arable land. This measure allowed the government to organize 200 state production units and the first cooperatives. In November 1979, Tomas Borge announced that more than 50% of arable land now belonged to the state and would be administered by the Nicaraguan Agrarian Reform Institute.

In 1981, an agrarian reform plan based on a mixed model combining a state enterprise system with agricultural cooperatives was in place, while in the months following the takeover of power 30% of the industrial sector was nationalized.[8] This public economic sector, called *Area de Propriedad del Pueblo* (People's Property Area or APP), controlled about 34% of GDP in 1980. Its development did not offend the private sector at a time when private financial institutions were bankrupt.

The agrarian policy also met with little opposition, since the expropriated lands were those of exiles or relatives of the dictatorship and it also made it possible to maintain agricultural exports, which was one of the government's priorities. It also appeared relatively moderate since the state agricultural sector began to decline after 1982 and the number of landless workers who received individual titles was very low.

This situation changed when the Sandinistas attacked medium-sized owners in 1982. All agricultural estates of more than 500 hectares on the Pacific coast and more than 1,000 hectares in the rest of the country were expropriated.[9] The change was spectacular. In a short time, Nicaragua's moderate agrarian reform plan became more radical and affected a majority of rural workers. The APP would account for 27.4% of the total farming area; the cooperative sector would take up 48.4%; small and medium-scale producers would account for 18.2%; and the large-scale producers would hold 6%. Between 1981 and 1984, 349 estates were expropriated.[10]

The beneficiaries of the agrarian reform also appeared disgruntled since the property titles were given collectively and not individually. This land distribution did not fit the mentality of farmers who wanted a division of the major areas where everyone would be the owner of a parcel. Moreover, the land that had been distributed could not be divided, sold or transferred before 1989. All of this caused only more disaffection amongst the peasantry. Despite many problems encountered in its implementation, access to credit for farmers had improved significantly and the land tenure system in Nicaragua became the most egalitarian throughout Latin America, with 75% of land owned by small and medium-sized producers.

Interference by the Sandinista state in economic life was not limited to the agricultural sector alone. As part of the Food Control and Regulation Policy in 1979, the Consumer Protection Act allowed it to regulate the prices of cereals and staple foods and to punish merchants who sold above the ceilings established by the authorities. In order to deepen these policies, between 1979-1982 the National Enterprise for Basic Foodstuffs (ENABAS) was created and strengthened and aimed to regulate the marketing and food distribution, an activity which quickly became a monopoly of the state. ENABAS set the prices, bought the products directly and distributed them all over the country. In 1983, it managed to capture almost 80% of the marketable production or 50% of total production. While ENABAS helped to ensure the population's access to basic products and for producers to earn a decent income, it displeased part of the peasantry who could no longer choose their customers and set their prices. Gradually, the Sandinistas' economic policy deeply affected the broad popular support for the anti-Somoza coalition. In some parts of the country, the land confiscation policy provoked anger among the population, particularly among the peasants of the Matagalpa, Boaco and Chontales departments, but also those of Nueva Segovia, Ocotal and Jinotega.

The Choice of the East

When they came to power, the Sandinistas chose not to take sides in the confrontation of the Cold War and favoured non-alignment, joining the organization of non-aligned countries in September 1979. If they did not want to get closer to the United States as the heir of Sandino, the man who fought against US imperialism and the Monroe doctrine, too close a rapprochement with the socialist camp made them fear to suffer the wrath of Washington as happened for Cuba from 1959.

Nicaragua's FSLN-led foreign policy could not be understood without recalling the role played by the United States in the region before and after 1979. Washington's influence in Nicaragua throughout the

20th century, and particularly under Somoza was equal to the hostility and bitterness of the Sandinistas towards the US. In these circumstances, the inexperience and blunders of the Sandinista leadership as well as the disproportionate US reactions led to a conflict whose repercussions extended beyond Nicaragua's borders.

The Carter administration, which could not prevent the FSLN from coming to power, viewed the new regime with suspicion. However, it wished to maintain a good relationship with Managua to prevent the Sandinistas from supporting the Salvadorian guerrillas and especially to prevent Nicaragua from switching to the Cuban and Soviet side. This benevolent approach would also allow Washington to retain some influence in promoting a pluralist democracy in the country. In order to influence the development of the situation in Nicaragua, Carter obtained from Congress the approval of a program of assistance.[11] Nevertheless, during a meeting with the Sandinistas in September 1979, he warned that this aid was conditional on Nicaragua's non-interference and attention to human rights and democracy. Nicaragua's abstention when the United Nations voted against the Soviet invasion of Afghanistan, the use of Cuban military advisers to organize the new Sandinista army, and their presence in large numbers during the 1980 literacy campaign, the resignation of non-Sandinistas from the JGRN, and the anti-US speeches of the Sandinista leaders were not well received. Above all, the Carter administration noted the links that were forged in March 1980 by Managua with the Soviet Union. Finally, in January 1981, when the CIA had evidence of Sandinista aid to the guerrillas in El Salvador, Carter suspended economic aid, ending his efforts to maintain good relations with Managua.

For their part, the Sandinistas assumed that a confrontation with the United States was inevitable, but they hoped to postpone it until their revolution was consolidated. That was why they did not openly challenge Washington as soon as they came to power, but sought to conclude trade agreements with new countries in order to reduce the country's dependence on the United States, and for that they turned to the socialist bloc. While Cuba had always supported the FSLN,

Decades of Somoza's dictatorship and natural catastrophes had wrecked Nicaragua: by 1980, the country was impoverished, yet full of abandoned arms. This little girl was photographed atop an abandoned Fiat CV.33 Ansaldo tankette, surrounded by several M3 half-tracks. (Albert Grandolini Collection)

Like Fidel Castro in Cuba 20 years earlier, the Sandinistas in Nicaragua also took time to make their minds up about the economic future of the country, and before opting to follow the way of Socialism. Once that decision was taken, a show-down with the US-supported opposition was inevitable. Taken in 1984, this photograph shows 'Supreme Leader' Fidel Castro with Daniel Ortega. (EPS, via Albert Grandolini)

particularly since 1978, the Soviet Union never had any contact with the Sandinistas until the fall of Somoza. This situation changed in 1979 when Moscow perceived that Nicaragua was a strategic area in the heart of Central America, while for Managua, the USSR could be a donor of funds and resources. Moscow therefore clearly announced on several occasions that it would support Nicaragua and as tensions between Managua and Washington continued to rise, the Soviets increased their commitment year after year.[12]

In March 1980, a first Nicaraguan delegation travelled to Moscow under the direction of Moises Hassan, a member of the JGRN.[13] Cooperation agreements were immediately signed with the USSR, Romania, East Germany and Czechoslovakia. Soon, the Soviet Union became the main supplier of goods, oil and arms for Nicaragua.[14] Aid from the socialist countries, which amounted to nearly $1 billion between 1979 and 1990, were essential for the implementation of Sandinista policies, curbing the impact of the economic crisis and hyperinflation and fighting domestic opponents.[15]

On the international scene, Sandinista Nicaragua could also count on the hostility of European countries towards US aggressive politics. France and Greece did not hesitate to sell arms, while Spain, which provided development aid to Nicaragua, made great efforts to promote a negotiated exit to the conflict affecting the country.

In Central American, Sandinista power contributed to the region's deep instability in the 1980s. It supported El Salvador's guerrillas and encouraged Guatemala's, while Honduras and Costa Rica formed the backbone of its opponents. The Sandinistas, however, initially benefited from the support of Panama, which sent military instructors to Managua. But at the end of 1979, Omar Torrijos, dissatisfied with the growing importance of Cubans in Nicaragua, decided to withdraw his advisers. Mexico, Venezuela, and Colombia, initially supportive of the Sandinistas, would quickly distance themselves to seek ways for a peace process for Central America.

The international situation in Nicaragua changed with the election of Ronald Reagan as President of the United States. The new president was a fierce anti-communist and an opponent of Détente. He therefore wanted the Sandinista regime to fall because of its ties with Cuba and the USSR, which he believed threatened US security, but also because he was convinced that Managua would seek to impose communism in the rest of Central America. For the new administration, the Nicaraguan question quickly became the symbol of its concept of the fight against communism, which was no longer satisfied with the containment applicable since the 1950s, but sought a rollback of communism. The promises of the Sandinista revolution of 1979 were far from being kept. If the economy was not socialized as on the Soviet and Cuban model, leaving a place for private companies, economic policy had made many dissatisfied both in the cities and the countryside. Politically, an opposition could continue to exist but within narrow limits and without the possibility of challenging the Sandinista monopoly on power. Internationally, while Managua maintained relations with many countries, particularly in Western Europe, it appeared as an ally of the Soviet bloc.

If the seizure of power by the Sandinistas and the socialist orientation of the economy laid the foundations for a civil war inside the country, Nicaragua also became the place of a collision between the two great powers in the context of a Cold War that was warming up in the first half of the 1980s. While the Soviet Union and its allies, mainly Cuba, supported the Sandinistas, the United States and other governments in the region chose to fight them, all of which were helping to prolong a civil war that would last nearly 10 years.

2
THE SANDINISTA FORCES

To understand the Sandinistas' rapport with the armed forces, it must not be forgotten that the FSLN was, before it seized power, a political and military organization whose armed struggle was a pillar. It was aware that an armed forces far removed from the revolutionary project ran a risk for the latter as shown by the example of Allende's Chile. Because of this, the armed forces of Sandinista Nicaragua could only be the instrument and the armed branch of the FSLN. One of the first measures taken by the JGRN after the victory of the revolution was therefore the formation of a permanent army closely controlled by the FSLN while the socialist idea of the armed people resulted in the formation of the Sandinista People's Militia (MPS).

The Birth of the EPS

In July 1979 the new government counted about 2,800 FSLN guerrillas and 15,000 fighters who joined the movement during the last months of the struggle against the dictatorship, but these fighters had no conventional military experience.[1] The Sandinistas could not rely on the remains of Somoza's army, the *Guardia Nacional* (GN) to build a new military force. The Fundamental Statute of the Republic decreed its dissolution and the officers and many GN NCOs were executed, exiled or imprisoned.[2] Without the support of an established military tradition and training system, the JGRN had to rely on foreign assistance.

The initial core of the EPS was formed by the cadre of the FSLN's revolutionaries and volunteers: most of the latter had joined the movement only in 1979. (Albert Grandolini Collection)

The United States, Panama and Venezuela offered their assistance but the offer was politely but firmly rejected.

The Sandinistas preferred to turn to Cuba and the USSR to build the new army of the country, a choice that indicated that they did not want to make it a neutral institution above the political quarrels but an instrument of their control over the country and power, a guarantee to continue the revolution in the direction desired by the National Directorate.

On 29 July, at a meeting at the Intercontinental Hotel in Managua, it was former guerrilla Joaquín Cuadra Lacayo who was appointed Chief of the General Staff.[3] In the same way, it was essentially the Sandinistas who formed the nucleus of the new army whose structure and command were defined by a decree of 22 August 1979. Humberto Ortega Saavedra was appointed commander-in-chief, Luis Carrión Cruz second in command, and Tomás Borge Martínez as Deputy Commander. In order to demonstrate the FSLN's hold on the army, the Decree of 22 August gave it the name the Sandinista People's Army (*Ejército Popular Sandinista* or EPS). The formation of this partisan army, in violation of the Puntarenas Pact, was completed at the end of 1979 when Bernardino Larios, a former GN officer, was replaced as Minister of Defence by Humberto Ortega, member of the FSLN National Directorate and already Commander-in-Chief of the EPS.[4]

The young EPS had at its creation only 12,500 poorly armed fighters with equipment taken from the GN and those available to the various fronts of the guerrillas.[5] The Armoured Battalion led by Javier Pichardo Ramírez took over the equipment of his GN predecessor with a tank company of M4 Shermans and Radial Stuarts, two armoured companies of T-17E1s, and transport. The first EPS artillery unit was also formed with material left by the GN: Israeli-made multiple rocket launchers, 60mm, 81mm, and 106mm mortars.

The majority of the FSLN's combatants were poorly-trained volunteers: eager to end Somoza's dictatorship, but ill-prepared to fight a conventional war. While including many females, and proving their mettle in clashes with the GN of 1978-1979 – when this photograph was taken – they subsequently had to be reorganized into a regular military. (Albert Grandolini Collection)

A platoon of EPS troops aboard a Unimog truck in 1980. By this time, most had received regular uniforms and black berets, but their primary armament remained FN FAL and H&K G3 assault rifles. (Albert Grandolini Collection)

To this armament was added that of the Southern Front: guns of 75mm, mortars of 60mm, 82mm, and 120mm.[6] In order to train professional soldiers, the EPS founded the Carlos Aguero School of Officers and the Walter Mendoza Military School. As early as the second half of 1979, an Engineering Battalion, a Communication Battalion, a Security Battalion to supervise military installations, and a Special Operations Unit were also formed.[7]

The wish to reform the country and create a new society, as well as fierce patriotism and opposition to US dominance prompted many young Nicaraguans to join the FSLN and then the EPS. At the same time, the FSLN was keen to establish and run the new armed forces as its military wing – which in turn required close links between the military and the public. (EPS via Albert Grandolini)

Even as of 1982, the EPS was still operating two companies equipped with T17E1 Staghound armoured cars, the crews of which also still used Israeli-made OR-201 kevlar helmets – as visible in this photograph. (Albert Grandolini Collection)

The US Threat

The forces available to the Sandinistas at the end of 1979 appeared to be very insufficient to defend the revolution against its potential adversaries. Informed by the Cuban example and by precedents in Nicaraguan history, Sandinista leaders feared above all US military intervention. To be able to deal with them, they decided to build a conventional army strong enough to deter Washington from attacking them directly. The Sandinistas wanted to force the United States, in the event of direct intervention, to use four divisions for its execution, a requirement that was difficult for Washington given its global commitments in the world.

The presence of US troops was increasingly important in Honduras, and the invasion of Grenada in October 1983 reinforced the strategy of Managua who feared to suffer the same fate as the Caribbean island. Within two months, trenches and defensive belts were built around Managua. This fear was also shared by Cuba, which withdraw the 2,000 teachers it had sent to Nicaragua.[8] Another alert occurred on the day of the second election victory of Reagan to the presidency in 1984 when the US media announcement of the arrival of Soviet jet fighters in Nicaragua was perceived by Managua as a justification for an impending invasion.[9]

According to Rafal del Pino, the Cubans established a common strategy with Humberto Ortega in the case of a US invasion of Nicaragua. As the Sandinistas had an army much more heavily equipped than that of the neighbouring states, the most modern forces would not be used to deal with the US invaders, who would be attacked by MPS forces as well as paramilitary units of the Ministry of the Interior.[10] At the same time, a Sandinista armoured column was expected to invade Costa Rica and take San Jose, the capital. All Cuban civilian advisers (already pre-organized into units) should join the military advisers and invade Honduras. Another Sandinista contingent was also expected to enter and cross Honduras and

Table 1: Military Regions of the Sandinista Forces, 1979-1982			
Military Zone	**RM**	**Headquarters**	**Provinces**
1st Military Zone			
	RM 1	Esteli	Estelí, Madriz, Nueva Segovia (HQ Esteli
	RM 2	Chinandega	León, Chinandega
independent	RM 4	Matagalpa	Matagalpa
independent	RM 5	Puerto Cabezas	Zelaya Norte, Puerto Cabezas, Rosita, Siuna, Bonanza
2nd Military Zone	RM 3	Managua	Managua
	RM 6	Granada	Carazo, Masaya, Granada, Rivas
	RM 7	Bluefields	Boaco, Chontales, Zelaya Central, Rio San Juan

The People's Militia (MPS) – much of which consisted of local youth, including these two young women photographed while taking a break during training – was to carry the burden of fighting US troops in the case of Washington ordering a military intervention in Nicaragua. (Albert Grandolini Collection)

then invade El Salvador. There, united with the forces of the Marti National Liberation Front, it should advance towards the Salvadoran capital and take it.[11]

Organization of the EPS

To organize the defence of the country, between 1979 and 1982 the Sandinista government, on the Cuban model, divided the country into *Region Militar* (Military Regions or RM) which each had a staff. Each RM was home to several EPS brigade headquarters in a particular geographic area. Some of the brigades inside the country had a regular army battalion but most of the forces were MPS and the members of the rural cooperatives that had been organized into MPS units of all kinds. Between 1982 and 1985, five RMs were grouped in two military zones.[12]

The Sandinista armed forces were divided into three branches: the ground troops of the EPS, the *Fuerza Aérea Sandinista y Defensa Antiaérea* (Sandinista Air Force-Air Force Defence or FAS-DAA) and the *Marina de Guerra Sandinista* (Sandinista Navy or MGS). Among these three branches, it was the EPS which formed the central axis around which the other two were developing. The EPS was organized into three levels: permanent troops, reserve troops and MPS.

The permanent troops were made up of professional soldiers who were divided into different types of units: armoured troops which formed the EPS strike force, artillery, air defence, infantry, troops of border guards.[13] In 1985, the permanent troops could gather 61,800 soldiers.[14]

The MPS were created on 21 February 1980 under the direction of Eden Pastora, then Deputy Minister of Defence. The MPS, which had 30,000 to 60,000 members in 1985, provided military training to the population, which could then be mobilized into the reserve troops. When they were active, these forces were under the control of the Ministry of Defence. The Commander of the Military Region exercised control over MPS units within his region through Brigade Commanders. From 1983 to 1990, there were 28 MPS brigades, each comprising four to six battalions.[15]

Militiamen were often government employees or Sandinista activists or supporters. They received basic military training on a few afternoons per month. Those who showed military ability were invited to join the Reserve Infantry Battalions. They received several weeks of full-time instruction and were allowed to return to their homes and workplaces to await the call of duty. There were 12,000 in 1985 and 30,000 in 1990. From 1982 onward, thousands were sent to fight under the orders of active officers of the EPS.[16]

Faced with the fear of US intervention and the emergence of an armed opposition within the country, volunteering no longer appeared sufficient to face all of these dangers. On 13 September 1983 the government introduced conscription with the *Servicio Militar Patriótico* (Military Patriotic Service or SMP). It concerned all Nicaraguan men aged 18 to 40 and women who volunteered; around 30% of the EPS strength was made up of women.[17]

Conscripts spent two years on active service, a period that could be extended by six months. After the age of 25, they were assigned to the Reserve until they turned 40. The majority of recruits, particularly from the Pacific region, belonged to battalions serving throughout the country, while in areas of conflict, they served locally in territorial infantry companies.[18]

However, there were several problems with the implementation of the SMP. First, there was the lack of a census to organize recruitment. Above all, there was the protest of the population, especially the conscripts' families; the EPS had to organize raids to recruit young people, which provoked demonstrations of anger as in the city of Nagarote in December 1984. In that month, FSLN recruiters knocked on doors to houses where they suspected that there were young people. Popular protest lead to uncontrolled riot.[19] The Church was also opposed to the SMP and among the first contingent of conscripts there was about 20% desertion.[20] The SMP, while increasing the number of EPS soldiers, quickly showed limitations. Towards the end of 1987 it became increasingly difficult to find new recruits since most of the generations concerned had already been mobilized. In the central mountainous regions, the SMP was a disaster and even promoted the recruitment of Contras since the ratio of peasants who had gone over to the Contras compared to those who were recruited by the revolutionary forces was five to one in favour of the Contras.[21]

Despite the difficulties of its implementation, the introduction of the SMP allowed the EPS to number about 60,000 men in 1984; six times more than the GN of Somoza at its peak. In addition, there were 60,000 militia members and a few tens of thousands of others with paramilitary training. In 1987, there were 74,000 active soldiers and 120,000 fighters with the reserve and the MPS.[22] The EPS then had 10 infantry battalions and one active airborne battalion and about

160 reserve and MPS infantry battalions. The recruitment effort supported by Cuban and Soviet aid allowed for the formation of the most powerful Central American armed force with conventional infantry units, armoured units and artillery brigades. Such an army nevertheless had an economic cost which resulted in a continuous increase of the military expenses. They thus increased from 20% of the national budget in 1980 to 46% in 1987.[23]

Cuban and Soviet Military Support

To support the construction of the Sandinista army in October 1979, Havana decided to send a military mission to Nicaragua. Its first leader was Colonel Fernando Fernández who was replaced in June 1983 by General Arnoldo Ochoa (the latter led Cuban troops in Angola and Ethiopia and enjoyed a prominent military reputation in Cuba).[24] His job was to bring his experience to the Sandinistas and help them develop a coherent military strategy to deal with the Contras and the US threat. With him, Cuba had also provided a number of veterans to organize the EPS and MPS. Their first mission was to train Sandinista officers, which allowed them to have a profound influence on the EPS, the organization of which largely followed the Cuban model. All military and strategic relations between Havana and Managua were headed by the Cuban Ambassador to Nicaragua, Julian Lopez Diaz, who was in fact Castro's personal representative in the country.[25]

Between about 500 and 800 Cuban military advisers were present in Nicaragua at all levels of the EPS, including the battalions.[26] In October 1985, Fidel Castro told Eduard Chevarnadze, the Soviet Minister of Foreign Affairs, that there were 700 Cuban military instructors in Nicaragua. There were in fact at most a thousand Cuban military advisers in Nicaragua at the same time, but this number was reduced in May 1986 so as not to gift any arguments to US propaganda.[27]

While the Cubans were mainly responsible for the tactical training of the EPS, Soviet soldiers, about 700 throughout the decade, were also present in Nicaragua, including those who maintained the military equipment provided to the EPS.[28]

Soviet military aid, while important, was no less modest in the beginning. According to the US authorities, the material sent to Nicaragua in 1979 was only $5 million and $6 to $7 million in 1980, which was only about the amount of aid granted by Washington to El Salvador. Military contacts were also established with the GDR in September 1979. East Berlin supplied equipment from 1980, including 15,000 AKM-8 submachine guns.[29] Czechoslovakia provided surface-to-air missiles, Bulgaria RPG-7 rocket launchers, Algeria anti-tank guns.[30]

Soviet aid took on a new dimension in May 1981, following Humberto Ortega's trip to Moscow. In June, an agreement was reached for the supply of heavy weapons and in July the first major Soviet military equipment arrived, which included armoured vehicles.[31] The main purpose of this equipment was to equip conventional Sandinista military forces around the Pacific coast to deal with the threat of a US invasion. After negotiations with Cuba in November 1981, a military assistance treaty was finally signed between Moscow and Managua.[32]

In 1981, Soviet military deliveries amounted to $39 to $45 million before rising to $80 million in 1982 and $110 million in 1983. But equipment delivered until 1983 most often consisted of small and basic weapons that were only useful for defence. The situation changed in 1983 with the signing of a secret plan between Managua, Havana and Moscow to increase Nicaragua's military potential.[33]

Soviet Armament in Nicaragua

In 1981, the first T-55 tanks arrived in Nicaragua to form the "Oscar Turcios Chavarria" armoured battalion stationed near Managua. It was composed of three tank companies, a mechanized company, an artillery group and an anti-aircraft defence group.[34] In 1982, the arrival of new T-55s made it possible to create a second armoured battalion. In 1984, the EPS had 110 T-55s organized in five armoured battalions of 22 tanks each. To date, the USSR had also provided 30 PT-76 light tanks, particularly suitable for difficult terrain.

Moscow also supplied BTR-60PB and BTR-152 armoured

Between 1981 and 1984, the EPS received a total of 110 T-55s. These were organized into five armoured battalions, each with 22 of these main battle tanks (MBTs). This T-55 belonged to the final batch delivered in 1984, and was photographed during a military parade in Managua, during the same year. (Albert Grandolini Collection)

personnel carriers from 1981 onwards, followed by amphibious BRDM-2 armoured reconnaissance vehicles, including some armed with 9M14 Malyutka (ASCC/NATO AT-3 Sagger) ATGMs. During the period 1983-1985, the arrival of this equipment allowed the EPS to create a mechanized brigade based in Villa Nueva with two tank battalions and a mechanized infantry battalion in RM 2. In RM 3 the 30th Mechanized Infantry Brigade was formed in Esquipulas with a tank battalion, mechanized infantry battalions and a motorized infantry battalion, and the 32nd Mechanized Infantry Brigade with two mechanized infantry battalions and a motorized infantry battalion. In 1985, the EPS had more than 200 armoured vehicles, most of them BTR-60PBs and BTR-152s.[35]

Table 2: Armoured Vehicles of the EPS, 1986[36]	
Type	Number of Vehicles
T-54/55	110
PT-76	25
BRDM-2	50 (some of which were armed with 9M14 Malyutka/AT-3 Sagger anti-tank missiles)
T17E1 Staghound	2
BTR-60PB	22
BTR-152	105

Thanks to Soviet aid, the EPS was well motorized with nearly 800 jeeps and about 3,500 IFA W.50 trucks supplied by East Germany and Libya. Material for the stewardship, communications, chemical decontamination, and tanker trucks were also delivered by socialist bloc countries. The EPS thus had a battalion of engineering and communication units.

Most of the artillery available to the EPS was also of Soviet origin. Moscow first delivered 57mm ZIS-2 anti-tank guns to Managua, and then in 1981 122mm D-30 and 152mm D-20 howitzers. In 1982, BM-21 multiple rocket launchers arrived in Nicaragua. The following year, the EPS had enough weapons to create the "Sergio Delgadillo Peña" artillery brigade.[37] Subsequently, artillery groups were formed in each RM. In 1987, the EPS had about 30 BM-21s, more than a hundred anti-tank guns and hundreds of mortars.[38]

The Sandinista Navy

The Sandinistas created a Navy on 13 August 1980, under the direction of Richard Lugo Kautz. It was composed of three naval squadrons based in Corinto, El Bluff and San Juan del Sur, and in 1985 the naval districts of the Pacific and Atlantic were formed.[39]

First equipped with modified fishing vessels, the Sandinista Navy bought two French Vedettes and two Soviet Zhuk patrol boats in 1982. The following year, it acquired two Kimjin patrol boats and two North Korean Sinhung torpedo boats, while Cuba delivered a Zhuk and two Yevgenya mine hunters in 1984 and the USSR offered four Polish-made K-8 mine hunters.[40] The Navy also had Griff guard boats, AIST flotilla boats, and two landing craft provided in 1984 by Spain.[41]

The FAS-DAA

In July 1979, the Sandinista Air Force had only a few aircraft inherited from the Somozist period, namely a few Cessna 337s, AT-33As and T-28s. In this sphere, everything had to be built; air bases had to be expanded and fortified, pilots and mechanics trained, and modern equipment acquired. To this end, Cuban Lt. Col. Rafael Fogueiras was sent by Havana to Managua where he became the head of the advisors attached to the FAS commanded by Major Raúl Venerio Granera.[42] Fogeiras was replaced in 1982 by Lt. Col. Diego Oquendo Ascención.

For pilot training, in 1980, Rafael Fogueiras ordered the selection of 30 young Nicaraguans, who, after a transit through Cuba to be assessed, were sent to Bulgaria for training.[43] For their equipment, the Soviets delivered some AN-2s, but these aircraft were old and obsolete. In 1982, Libya provided six SF.260ML/W light training aircraft that could also be armed and the USSR supplied two AN-26 transport aircraft.

The secret agreement between Moscow, Havana and Managua

The second tank-type to enter service was the PT-76 – a lightly armoured amphibious tank with a 76mm main gun – of which about 30 were delivered in the early 1980s. (Albert Grandolini Collection)

Infantry of the sole EPS mechanised battalion – based in Villa Nueva – which was equipped with BTR-60PB armoured personnel carriers (APCs). These could carry up to 14 troops, and were armed with a 14.5mm heavy machine gun mounted in a turret. (Albert Grandolini Collection)

Through 1982 and 1983, the mechanised formations of the EPS also received BRDM-2 armoured reconnaissance vehicles. This pair was photographed during a parade in Managua in 1985. (US DoD)

allowed for an increase in military aid to Nicaragua. Above all, it provided for the delivery of 16 MiG-21Bis, scheduled for 1984. The agreement also included the delivery of radars, a squadron of ten Mi-17 helicopters, three AN-26s, and two S-125 (SA-3 Goa) batteries. The delivery of the MiG-21s had to pass through Cuba, in order not to give the impression that the USSR had supplied them directly to Managua. It was planned to assemble them in Cuba, paint them in Sandinista colours and then fly them directly from Cuba to Nicaragua, with a stopover in Puerto Cabezas. During their flight, the MiGs were reportedly guided by a Tu-154 of the *Cubana de Aviación*. To make the operation possible, it was necessary to extend the Puerto Cabezas Air Base runway so that the MiGs could land and take off again. The extension was completed in early 1985. However, the Soviets became more cautious after Brezhnev's death, and the delivery of the MiGs was finally cancelled.[44] The USSR did not want to provoke an excessive reaction from Washington, especially when the Reagan Administration stated that if Nicaragua obtained MiGs, it would be forced to launch an attack to destroy them.[45]

To offset the lack of aircraft, the Sandinistas sought to build a solid fleet of combat helicopters. In 1981, Moscow sent two Mil Mi-8 (ASCC/NATO-codename 'Hip') to Nicaragua. This helicopter had enabled the army to evacuate wounded soldiers, carry ammunition and other supplies to remote outposts and move combat units quickly. It was equipped with air-to-ground rockets, and some models carried machine guns in the nose. It could carry 32 people and cruise at speeds up to 250km per hour. In 1982, Managua acquired two Aerospatiale SA.316B Alouette III helicopters from France and two Mi-2/Hoplite training helicopters.

At the end of 1984, the Soviets delivered to Managua, via Bulgaria, the first modern combat helicopters, the Mi-25/HIND. This helicopter, used by the Soviets in Afghanistan, proved to be a decisive weapon in the fight against the Contra forces from 1985 onwards.[46] By 1986, Managua had received a total of 14 Mi-8 and 30 Mi-17 assault helicopters, and 12 Mi-25 gunships: thus, within just two years – from 1984 until 1986 – the FAS tripled its stock of Soviet-made rotary wing aircraft.[47] After the final batch of six arrived in 1986, the Mi-25 fleet reached its peak strength in early 1987. The Mi-8s, Mi-17s, and Mi-25s were regularly operating from up-country airfields, including San José de Bocay. Operational rates were high enough that, for most of 1987 the new FAS commander Lieutenant-Colonel Javier Pichardo Ramirez (former military chief in the western provinces of Leon and Chinandega), rarely had fewer than 40 helicopters – mostly Mi-17s – at his disposal.[48]

The first FAS combat mission took place on 15 September 1979, providing fire support to small EPS units on the Zapotal River, in Ocotal and then in the Santa María, Ococona, Nueva Segovia region with three Push-Pulls. This participation in the fighting increased in the following years. In 1985, Mi-25 support helicopters were first used against the attack on La Trinitad by the Contras.

For air transport, the FAS used US-made helicopters (H-500, S-58-T Sikorski, UH-1H) until 1983. With the arrival of Soviet helicopters in 1984, air detachments were created in the 1st, 5th, 6th and 7th RMs to provide support to ground units, carry out aeromedical evacuations, and provide transport for troops and equipment.[49]

With the help of the Cubans and Soviets, the Sandinistas were building the infrastructure needed to organize and deploy modern aviation. In 1982, the construction of the Punta Huete air base, called "El Panchito", in the north-east of Managua began. It was Fidel Castro who approved a $60 million loan for the construction of this base designed by Cuban and Soviet engineers. It had a runway and

Table 3: Aircraft and Helicopters of the FAS, 1980-1988[53]	
Type	Number of Available Airframes
Aerospatiale SE.316B Alouette III	2
Antonov An-2	6
Antonov An-26	2
Bell UH-1C	2
CASA C.212A	2
Cessna 337	9
Cessna 180	2
Hughes 300	1
Hughes OH-6A	2
IAI.201 Arava	1
Lockheed AT-33A	3
Mil Mi-2 (ASCC/NATO-codename 'Hoplite')	2
Mil Mi-8/17 (ASCC/NATO-codename 'Hip')	44
Mil Mi-25 (ASCC/NATO-codename 'Hind')	12
North American T-28A	2
SIAI-Marchetti SF.260	6 (2 operational on average)
Sikorsky S.58T	3 (1 operational on average)

Table 4: Known Serial Numbers of FAS Mi-8s, Mi-17s and Mi-25s		
Type	Serial Number	Notes
Mi-8T	264	
Mi-8T	265	crashed 9 Dec 1982
Mi-8T	269	crashed 19 Jul 1986
Mi-8T	270	shot down 2 Dec 1985
Mi-8T	272	
Mi-8T	274	
Mi-8T	281	shot down 29 Oct 1987
Mi-8T	282	
Mi-17	282	shot down 20 Sep 1987
Mi-8T	283	
Mi-8T	284	
Mi-17	284	badly damaged and abandoned 16 Jan 1986
Mi-17	285	
Mi-17	287	damaged by ground fire 16 Jan 1986; shot down 12 Jun 1987
Mi-8T	289	
Mi-17	289	
Mi-17	290	
Mi-8T	293	
Mi-8T	293	crashed 4 Nov 1986
Mi-17	294	crashed 30 Oct 1986
Mi-17	301	crashed 25 Jan 1987
Mi-17	302	crashed 17 Sep 1986
Mi-17	303	
Mi-17	305	shot down 11 Oct 1987
Mi-17	307	shot down 27 Aug 1987
Mi-17	315	
Mi-17	316	crashed 14 Oct 1987
Mi-17	317	
Mi-17	318	damaged in collision with 321 30 Jul 1999
Mi-17	321	crashed 30 Jul 1999
Mi-17	322	
Mi-17	328	
Mi-25	338	
Mi-25	339	
Mi-25	340	
Mi-25	341	damaged by FAH SMB.2 17 Mar 1988
Mi-25	354	
Mi-25	355	flown to Honduras, 8 Dec 1988; returned in 1989
Mi-25	359	
Mi-25	361	
Mi-25	362	
Mi-25	363	

equipment capable of receiving all types of aircraft in service in Eastern Bloc air forces.[50] The Sandino International Airport in Managua was modernized as were those of Montelimar, Puerto Cabezas, Estelí, La Rosita and Bluefield. The construction of these bases was a constant source of concern for Washington who feared they would be used to enable the Soviet air force to operate in the Western Pacific and on the west coast of the United States.[51]

In order to protect Nicaragua's skies, in 1983 the USSR provided an Early Warning/Ground Control Intercept (EW/GCI) system that was installed near Masaya. This allowed the creation of the Radio

The FAS began small, using the miscellany of aircraft left behind from the former Fuerza Aerea (de) Nicaragua (FAN). Amongst these was a pair of Cessna 180s. By 1980, both of these were camouflaged (apparently in tan and dark green), received serials 53 and 57, and were soon armed with French-made Matra F1 pods for unguided 68mm rockets. (Pit Weinert Collection)

Another view of the Cessna 180 serial number 53. Notable is the official insignia of the FAS as in use during the early 1980s, including the service title and two strips in national colours (red and black) on the fin. Also notable is the service title applied on the undersurface of the left wing, and the LAU-3 launcher (or US origin) on the example in the foreground. (Pit Weinert Collection)

Two other types inherited by the FAS from the former FAN were the T-28 (foreground, right), and the AT-33A. These two were photographed while put on display – together with representative armament, including 68mm and 127mm unguided rockets – for top commanders of the EPS in 1981. (Pit Weinert Collection)

Technical Troops under the command of Captain Francisco Figueroa. In 1984 other radars were installed in Toro Blanco and Estelí and in 1985 in San Juan del Sur. In 1984, a radar surveillance system was installed in Polvon to control the Atlantic coast. Thanks to this surveillance system, the EPS radars covered the whole country and also part of Honduras, El Salvador and Costa Rica.

This surveillance system made it possible to organize anti-aircraft defence forces first of all with ZPU-4, ZU-23-2 and M-1939 anti-aircraft guns. On the ground, the EPS used Man-Portable Air Defence (MANPADs), foremost Soviet-made Strela (ASCC-Code SA-7 Grail). In 1984, 100mm KS-19 guns with radar control were added. Nearly 400 anti-aircraft guns and about 350 SA-7 and SA-14 (the successor to the SA-7) ground-to-air missiles protected Nicaragua's skies.[52]

Sandinista Security Forces

Besides the EPS, the Sandinista government also had a security apparatus in order to fight its opponents. In July 1979, the Ministry of the Interior (MINT) was entrusted to Tomás Borge Martínez who built the Sandinista security apparatus with the cooperation of different countries such as the USSR, the GDR, Bulgaria, Czechoslovakia, Poland, Hungary, as well as Cuba. The security forces were then divided into two branches. There was the Sandinista police led by René Vivas Lugo who was in charge of public order and the fight against delinquency and crime. This police force was a model compared to those of other countries in the region by dint of its professionalism and its refusal of corruption, and was well regarded by the population.[54]

The second branch was formed by the General Directorate of State Security (DGSE) headed by a relative of Humberto Ortega, Lénin Cerna Juárez. The DGSE, supported by Cuban and East German advisers, oversaw and repressed the entire population with brutal methods, particularly those who may have had links with the Somoza regime and then the Contras. The repression was justified by the need to fight Somozism and first and foremost the remains of the GN. On 3 October 1979, the Permanent Commission on Human Rights (PCHR) denounced the cases of imprisonment and disappearance of former GNs and the existence of mass graves near Granada. While Borge replied that they were victims of uncontrolled

A Sandinista Police officer. Reasonably well-trained and equipped, they were soon to see combat in action against the *Counterrevolutionaries* (or 'Contras'). (Albert Grandolini Collection)

The MINT was responsible for creating the first – and perhaps the best – counterinsurgency (COIN) asset of the Nicaraguan armed and police forces, the *Tropas Pablo Ubeda* (TPU), in July 1979. Trained by Vietnamese advisors, troops of this unit (some of the first in Nicaragua after 1979 to wear camouflage fatigues) were the equivalent to the Long-Range Surveillance units of the US Army, capable of infiltrating enemy positions or running attacks on enemy bases in the rear. (Albert Grandolini Collection)

violence, the CPHD denounced more than 600 disappearances in Granada between July 1979 and July 1980 as well as the existence of illegal detention centres. Subsequently, this repression was carried out against the opponents who were included in the category of counter-revolutionaries.

The DGSE's action was particularly effective since it prevented the Contras from making multiple attempts to move the conflict to cities in the Pacific region. To this end, it had about 3,000 personnel and operated mainly behind the fronts and in the cities, including Managua. In rural areas, it sometimes carried out executions and formed a network of informants. It thus managed to infiltrate the Contras, where some of its members were discovered but others managed to remain infiltrated until 1990. It also infiltrated opposition parties. It relied on the entire network of CDSs, AMNLAE, Young Sandinistas, pioneers and other mass organizations controlled by FSLN. If the DGSE was brutal, using torture and inhuman treatment, these acts of violence never reached the same proportions as those of the countries in the region engaged in counter-insurgency struggles.

Pilots and ground personnel of the FAS AT-33As, as seen at Sandino IAP, in the early 1980s. Notable is the original camouflage pattern (consisting of tan, green and dark green), the initial national insignia (with letters 'F' and 'S' in red, and 'A' in black), and the service title. Subsequently replaced by SF.260s and then Mi-25s, the last three Nicaraguan AT-33As were to undergo at least two additional re-paintings before their withdrawal from service. (Albert Grandolini Collection)

Hysteria over Nicaraguan 'MiGs'

Time and again during the 1980s, the government in Washington would publish 'alarming news' about the 'massive Nicaraguan military build-up', the extension of diverse airfields in Nicaragua, and especially: either 'expected' or even 'confirmed deliveries of Soviet-made MiG-21 fighter-bombers'. Eventually, the Sandinistas never acquired any MiGs – which would be ill-suited for the kind of operations they ran against the Contras, anyway. Nevertheless, after being donated six SIAI-Marchetti SF.260Ws, they almost acquired Czechoslovak-made Aero L-39 Albatross training jets with combat capability – from Libya.

On 21 April 1983, one of a formation of three Ilyushin Il-76 transports of the Libyan Arab Air Force experienced technical problems and all were forced to land in Brazil. An inspection by the Brazilian authorities revealed that while their cargo was officially declared as 'medical supplies', they actually carried the first of 17 L-39s planned to be delivered to Managua by Tripoli, together with their arms, spares, and parachutes for their future pilots. According to the FAS Colonel Ricardo Wheelock Roman, the Sandinista Command had no previous knowledge of this shipment. After being impounded in Brazil for some time, all of the Il-76s – and their cargo – were returned to Libya.

Libyan Il-76s as seen while impounded in Brazil. (Albert Grandolini Collection)

Libya did manage to deliver six SIAI-Marchetti SF.260Ws to Nicaragua in the early 1980s, and the type entered service with the FAS. However, lack of spares and availability of other aircraft and helicopters resulted in all of these ending up in 'open storage'. This photograph was taken in 1982. (Pit Weinert Collection)

The MINT also had special forces, the TPU (*Tropas Pablo Ubeda*) created in July 1979, a militarized unit used for combined force operations coordinated with the military. It was trained by the Vietnamese and specialized in infiltration and the destruction of enemy bases. One of their best-known operations was the infiltration and destruction of the ARDE camp at El Corozo in November 1984.[55]

At the judicial level, since the end of 1979 repression could be based on the nine special courts created to deal with the former GNs. Later, during the fight against the Contras, the authorities formed the Anti-Somozist People's Tribunals, exceptional courthouses where the rights of the defence were often violated.[56]

If the Sandinista armed forces were created on the hypothesis of facing a US invasion on the model of the operation against Grenada in 1983 or the Bay of Pigs against Cuba in 1961, the real threat was soon different to what was imagined. Instead of a confrontation with conventional forces, the EPS had to fight irregular formations practicing guerrilla warfare. This forced it to review its structure and its military doctrine to stand up to them.

This clandestinely-taken photograph shows the military side of the Sandino International Airport (IAP) as of 1982. Visible are one of the first two Mi-8s delivered to Nicaragua (left upper corner), one of the last remaining Sikorsky S-58s (centre, right), and one T-28 Trojan (centre, bottom). (Albert Grandolini Collection)

3

THE BIRTH OF THE CONTRAS (1980-1982)

The policy pursued by the Sandinistas after they came to power led to the advent of different opposition groups. Some were peaceful like those of the Catholic Church or the Civil Opposition, others resorted to the armed struggle like that of the central region's peasants, the Atlantic region natives and those nostalgic for Somoza's dictatorship. These opposition groups had different roots, and different objectives, but for the Sandinista government they formed a threat that was included under the term of *contrarrevolucionarios* (counter-revolutionary) or Contras.

Civil Opposition and ex-GN

The FSLN's hold on power quickly provoked reactions and opposition. If the Sandinistas controlled all the levels of power, they had to face a powerful institution in Nicaragua, the Catholic Church. The latter, who supported the FSLN during the fight against Somoza, changed their attitude in the early years of the revolutionary government, particularly because of the growth, with the support of the power, of the popular church which professed a theology of liberation against the ecclesiastical hierarchy and the presence of several radical priests in the government.[1] This Catholic opposition increased with the election as pope of John Paul II. The latter showed a more aggressive anti-communism as Nicaragua approached the socialist camp and especially condemned the theology of liberation. In May 1980, the Vatican asked that priests occupying positions in the administration resigned; only four refused. Cardinal Miguel Obando y Bravo quickly became confrontational with the government and John Paul II's visit to Nicaragua in 1983 did not improve the situation.[2]

Politically, the resignation of Alfonso Róbelo and Violeta Chamorro less than a year after the fall of Somoza brought to light the end of the anti-Somoza coalition. If Violeta Chamorro then took over the management of the newspaper *La Prensa*, Róbelo's efforts to transform the MDN into a major opposition party failed and he finally left the country. Róbelo's departure was a shock to the private economic sector. The opposition to the Sandinistas was embodied in the *Consejo Superior de la Empresa Privada* (Higher Council of Private Enterprises or COSEP), the country's main employer group.

COSEP worried about the deterioration of the economic situation and called for the end of the expropriation policy.[3] But its main grievances against the FSLN were political; it called for the end of the state of emergency, for the guarantee of private property and for freedom of expression. If it did not express it openly, COSEP criticized above all the Sandinistas' failure to leave the private sector a place to exert an influence, and denounced the non-compliance with the agreements of Puntarenas. The FSLN reaction was brutal. In October 1980, when COSEP wrote to Daniel Ortega to demand accountability for the economic situation, the government arrested the signatories of the letter. The reinforcement of exchange control in September 1981 introduced a state of economic and social exception under which several leaders of COSEP were imprisoned. But the Sandinistas did not want a break with the private sector and they took care to distinguish between a "patriotic bourgeoisie" and "traitors to the homeland", emphasizing that the first had a role to play in the economic sphere.[4]

During the rest of the decade, COSEP remained the private sector's representative in the country and embodied the civil opposition to the Sandinista regime. Its positions were relayed in public by the largest newspaper of Nicaragua *La Prensa* directed by Violeta Chamorro, for which reason the government created its own daily newspaper, *Barricada*, directed by the son of Violeta, the journalist Carlos Fernando Chamorro.[5]

Some COSEP members were radicalized, like Jorge Salazar

The anti-Sandinista movement was able to fall back upon the support of anti-Castrist Cubans of the Independence and Democracy for Cuba Movement, led by Huber Matos (centre of the photo). (Albert Grandolini Collection)

Arguello, President of the Union of Producers Agricultural Workers of Nicaragua and Vice-President of COSEP. Salazar was anti-Somozist and in July 1979 he collaborated with the FSLN. Gradually, especially in the face of the government's agrarian policy, he went into opposition and in July 1980 he was convinced that the civil opposition to Sandinism was insufficient to stop the Marxist path that the country took. He tried to convince influential politicians of the need to organize an armed opposition. He was then approached by Nestor Moncada who announced that he represented a group of EPS officers who wanted to overthrow the Sandinistas. The two men met on several occasions. Salazar tried to rally supporters, especially in business circles, and travelled abroad to present his plans to anti-Sandinista exiles such as former colonel of the GN, Enrique Bermúdez, or José Francisco Cardenal, the former president of the construction industry. Conversations with Moncada continued, but he was actually working for the DGSE. In November 1980, after a new encounter, Salazar was shot dead in a neighbourhood of Managua.[6] The Sandinista media accused him of organizing a plot. Salazar's death was a shock for the opposition and steered many opponents to think that only the armed struggle was effective against the Sandinistas.

The question of the choice of armed struggle did not arise for former Somoza supporters and ex-GN members. The FSLN, by refusing to integrate the ex-GNs into the new army, despite the demands of the United States and Costa Rica, pushed them to flee to Miami and Honduras where they quickly organized themselves. Groups were formed in the summer of 1979, such as *Los Zebras* in Honduras under the direction of Ricardo Lau, the *Ejército de Liberación Nacional* (National Liberation Army or ELN), the *Alianza Democrática Revolucionaria Nicaragüense* (ARDEN) or in Costa Rica the *Union Democratica Revolucionaria Nicaraguense-Fuerzas Armadas Revolucionarias de Nicaragua* (UDN-FARN) by Pedro Chamorro Rapacciolli.[7]

In Honduras, Pablo Emilio Salazar, Commander Bravo, quickly became the leader of these exiles. A charismatic leader, he founded the Nicaraguan Refugee Assistance Committee in Honduras, which was more of a small army than a humanitarian organization. Faced with the danger it represented, a Sandinista commando led by Lenin Cerda organized his kidnapping in Tegucigalpa on 10 October 1979, and killed him. When Borge announced the death of Salazar he used the term "Contras" for the first time.

Other ex-GNs who lived in Guatemala were organized into the *Légion 15 de Septiembre* (Legion 15th September) which was founded on 31 December 1979 during a meeting in Tegucigalpa. Initially, its members organized military training before being trained directly by Guatemalan soldiers. In March 1980, the Legion, still with the support of the Guatemalan army, moved to the border between Honduras and Nicaragua and began small raids into Jalapa department to recover weapons.

At the head of the Legion was former Colonel Enrique Bermúdez, who was Nicaragua's military attaché in Washington in the 1970s. The Legion quickly established links with other groups in Guatemala and Costa Rica and raised money from exiles to buy small arms. Among these members was former FAN colonel Emilio Echeverry, a friend of General Gustavo Álvarez who commanded the Honduran police forces and agreed to support the Legion.[8]

In April 1981, Álvarez met William Casey, the director of the CIA, to ask him for US support in the anti-Sandinista struggle. Casey was cautious and if he agreed to provide funds he did not want to send US military instructors to the Legion. For this Álvarez turned to Argentina where he had studied and had many contacts.[9]

Argentina, which was a loyal supporter of Somoza Debayle, was at that time a major player in secret anti-communist operations in Latin America.[10] Bermúdez therefore went to Buenos Aires and Videla's dictatorship agreed to train Legion officers and send instructors to Honduras. The Argentine government saw the Legion as a force it could use to attack left-wing movements in Central America. In exchange for material support, the Legion became an instrument of the Argentine dictatorship when, for example, it was used to attack a radio station in Costa Rica that was broadcasting programmes attacking the Argentine government.[11] It seemed that Washington had agreed to Argentine involvement with the Legion.[12]

With the help of Álvarez, the Legion was increasing its presence in southern Honduras near the Nicaraguan border where, as part of the Ariel project, it was setting up camps and training centres called *Ariel*, *Zebras*, *Sagitario*, *Agateite*, *Arenales*, and *Pino I* and where 234 fighters had settled.[13] Later on, *Fenix* camp was also created near the Atlantic region to train the Miskito, Sumo and Rama Indians.[14]

Legion officers were trained by the Argentinians, such as the *Batallón de Inteligencia 601* at the El Epaterique school, while the whole was financed by the US to the tune of around $15 million in 1981-1982.[15] Argentines also relied on anti-Castro Cubans from Miami to obtain funds and purchase weapons from Taiwan, Thailand and South Korea to arm the Contras.[16]

In April 1981, the various anti-Sandinista groups met in Guatemala City to unite their forces within the Nicaragua Democratic Force (FDN), which included the former GN of the Legion 15th September. Some time later in Fort Lauderdale, Florida, Orlando Bolaños was appointed military commander and Enrique Bermúdez, number two.

The formation of the FDN marked a turning point in the history of the Contras. Bringing together former Somozist soldiers and anti-Sandinista civilians, it offered a political and military alternative to the Sandinista project. Nevertheless, in 1981, the FDN remained a small organization. It in no way represented a threat to the Sandinista regime since it had only gathered 437 ex-GN soldiers by August 1982.[17] This situation changed radically when Washington, after the withdrawal of the Argentinians following their defeat in the Falklands war, decided to massively support the Contras and part of the Nicaraguan population rose up against the Sandinistas.

The Atlantic Coast Uprising

For a long time, the Atlantic region of Nicaragua was neglected by the authorities. The demographic and economic heart of the country was the Pacific coast, which accounted for 61% of its 2.7 million inhabitants according to the 1980 census, while the Atlantic region had only 10%. These two regions lived with their backs to one another. The Matagalpa-Puerto Cabezas road, which crossed the country from coast to coast, was only opened under the presidency of Somoza Debayle. This separation was not only geographical but also ethnic and cultural, the result of Nicaragua's history. The Atlantic coast was inhabited by Miskito, Sumu and Rama Indians, as well as Creoles of African origin and Spanish-speaking mixed race. Long under British rule, Protestantism was present there through the Evangelical Churches and the Moravian Church. The Miskitos also had their own language, while the black population used Creole derived from English.

The central government had always neglected this region and its demographic and economic marginality had never made it a worry for Managua. A modus-vivendi had gradually been established with the central government: the latter exploited the region's mineral and forest resources and left to relative autonomy the community organizations that applied traditional customs.[18] This mutual indifference explained why the people of the region did not participate in the anti-Somoza uprising of the late 1970s.

When it came to power, the FSLN wanted to transform the region to integrate it into the national whole and to this end it conducted an active policy. Before 1979, contacts were established with the Alliance for the Progress of Miskitos and Sumos (ALPROMISU) founded in 1973 and led by two Miskitos who studied in Managua, Steadman Fagoth Müller and Brooklyn Rivera Bryan. They began to collaborate with the Sandinistas, believing that the revolution opened up an opportunity for the population's demands for self-government.

The first MISURA units depended on ambushing Sandinista patrols to obtain automatic assault rifles of the AKM series – and they included at least as many female combatants as their enemy. (Albert Grandolini Collection)

In eastern, underdeveloped and poorly populated parts of Nicaragua, the opposition had it relatively easy to recruit amongst the indigenous populations of the Miskito and Summo – even more so from up to 15,000 Indios that found refuge in Honduras. (Albert Grandolini Collection)

Fagoth was thus appointed as a representative to the Council of State. But the differences between the indigenous peoples of the Atlantic coast, on the one hand, and the Sandinista government, on the other, quickly became apparent.

The activist policy pursued by the new authorities quickly led to mistrust in the region. The ubiquity of FSLN appointed people in the administration, mainly from the Pacific coast, the non-respect of the Indian communities' customary rights and the desire to impose the Spanish language were causing anger.[19] Above all, EPS troops – about 7,000 men – settled in the main cities. Its presence was perceived as that of an occupying force and was denounced as "internal colonialism."[20] Anger in the Atlantic region also had a religious basis. The Moravian Church was important there and this Church was firmly anti-communist. Agrarian policy also increased discontent when the Sandinistas took over community land to set up state plantations producing sugar cane or palm oil for export.

The Indian leaders who were still demanding more autonomy then founded MISURASATA, an acronym which in Miskito means "Miskito, Sumo, Rama, Sandinista All Together" to replace ALPROMISU.[21] For its part, the Managua government wanted to hold the Atlantic coast as the first Contra groups began to operate in the northern highlands and along the border with Honduras. Incidents were increasing in the region. Thus, in September 1980, a riot broke out in Bluefields where popular anger was caused by the presence of Cubans, as shown by banners such as "The Atlantic coast demands justice without communism."[22] The crowd also demanded independence and occupied the city's airport.[23] This was the first major popular anti-Sandinista demonstration in the country and these incidents led to numerous arrests and excessive repression by the EPS in 1980 and early 1981.

In January 1981, Fagoth announced the beginning of the "political war" of MISURASATA against the FSLN. The riots of Puerto Cabezas in February 1981, then in the rest of the region, definitively marked the split between MISURASATA and the FSLN. The authorities who wanted to put an end to the separatist attempts banned MISURASATA and arrested Fagoth on 21 February, who, once released, found refuge in Honduras while the rest of the organisation settled in Costa Rica.[24] In March and April 1981, thousands of Miskitos who feared the consequences of the repression began to flee to Honduras across the Rio Coco River.[25] Armed groups were forming in Honduras that launched raids against the Sandinista garrisons, resulting in reprisals against villagers accused of complicity with them. The population of the Atlantic coast was then divided between those who advocated negotiation with the FSLN and those who chose armed struggle.

Under Fagoth's leadership, MISURA was formed in Honduras, which established a staff, a political commission and a Council of Elders, the supreme authority for Indians in exile. In August 1981, after the integration of MISURA into the FDN, the Honduran army opened the first training camps for the Miskitos. Some received specific training from the Honduran army, and sometimes even from Guatemalan or Argentinean officers.[26]

The MISURA forces, under the leadership of a former GN, Nicodemo Serapio, launched the *Red Christmas* campaign at the end of 1981 by launching attacks in the Raiti area, on the border of the Atlantic region and the Jinotega department. Supported by the inhabitants, they ambushed the Sandinista patrols in order to obtain their first automatic weapons. On the strength of these initial successes, they attacked various small garrisons. Excited by these first strikes and strengthened by their new firepower, Serapio and his staff seized the military post installed in Raiti and occupied the village on 6 and 7 December 1981, before attacking San Carlos on 14 December, when they butchered all the members of the garrison.

These first military operations marked a turning point since they inaugurated a merciless fight between the MISURA guerrillas and the Sandinistas. In reaction to this *Red Christmas*, the Sandinistas responded with brutality. They launched a counter-offensive in the area of Raiti and San Carlos between 22 to 26 December and took revenge for their losses by massacring dozens of Miskitos miners in Leimus.[27]

The FSLN, which did not want to lose control of the situation in an area close to two borders, launched a population displacement programme in early 1982, particularly in the areas bordering Honduras. Once the areas were emptied of inhabitants, EPS burned down houses, destroyed abandoned villages and took away livestock. The 8,500 displaced people settled in five camps 70km from the border and west of Puerto Cabezas. Subsequently, the Sandinistas again expelled 7,000 Miskitos who lived near the Rio Coco in the Jinotega department and settled them in coffee plantations in the Matagalpa department. This policy led to radicalization of the Miskitos and protests from the Church and foreign governments denouncing human rights violations.

As a result of these displacement operations, tens of thousands of Miskitos fled to Honduras where they were welcomed by the MISURA and then taken charge of by the Office of the United Nations High Commissioner for Refugees. In 1984, more than 15,000 Miskitos were in refugee camps in Honduras.[28] These operations also meant that the US, who until then had given minimal aid to the Miskito exiles, would provide them with significant support and took them into account in their strategy to contain the Sandinista revolution.

The Uprising in the Central Regions

A similar reaction to that of the Atlantic region affected the central mountainous area of the country, namely the departments of Boaco, Chontales, Matagalpa and Jinotega. These regions had long formed a pioneering front where many landless peasants from the Pacific region settled, particularly since the 1950s. Unlike the Pacific zone where export agriculture dominated in large estates, the *latifundia*, with its landlords and proletariat of agricultural workers, the highlands of the central part of the country form a "Peasant Country". The pioneer farmers who cleared land and built their farms formed a rural middle-class based on a modest and frugal but independent way of life. The most successful, the *finqueros*, dominated the rural life of these communities and organized solidarity networks.

The arrival of the Sandinistas in power quickly threatened this individualist way of life, particularly through the rural policy. While the agrarian reform initially affected the large landowners linked to the Somoza clan, Decree No. 782 of July 1981, which authorized the expropriation of land of more than 1,000 hectares, had a wider scope.[29] It affected sharecroppers and small landowners and generated a huge contradiction in rural communities. The FSLN made the mistake of thinking that in the countryside there were two opposing social classes: the exploited peasants and an exploiting bourgeoisie, without considering that in the rural areas of the central regions, there was a network of complex social, economic and family relations. Above all, the arrival of the Sandinistas disrupted traditional hierarchies, calling into question the status and authority of the finqueros.[30] Dissatisfaction grew among the rural communities of Matagalpa and Jinotega, who had often been actively involved in the fight against Somoza and as a result, felt betrayed.

The peasants organized themselves into the MILPAS, the Anti-Sandinista Popular Militias, formed first to fight Somoza before the revolution under the name of Anti-Somozist Popular Militias. Their first action took place in El Chipote near Quilali in November 1979 with an attack on a EPS camp.[31] The first structured MILPAS troop was formed by Pedro Joaquín González alias "Dimas" with about thirty former guerrillas from Quilalí and Wiwilí. González came from a wealthy family of coffee farmers before joining the FSLN and fighting under the command of German Pomares. In 1979, he became an officer of the EPS in Quilalí and then turned against the FSLN, accusing it of betraying the revolution. This was also the case of Encarnación Baldivia Chavarria alias "El Tigrillo", a peasant from the Jinotega region who joined the FSLN as a guerrilla and became an officer after the revolution. He quickly deserted to join "Dimas."[32]

In December 1979, González met in Managua with members of the civil opposition such as Jorge Salazar and Alfonso Robelo, who gave him the task of forming a guerrilla group in the north of the country. But contacts were soon broken. In search of support, the MILPAS turned to Honduras but received no assistance from the ex-GN.[33] In early 1980, they organized a training camp in El Caracol on the banks of the Rio Coco. The fighters were only supplied by the finqueros and received weapons through sympathetic militiamen.[34]

On 23 July 1980, the MILPAS attacked the small town of Quilalí, taking over the army headquarters, the police station and the Sandinista agricultural union office before quickly withdrawing.[35] The authorities' reaction was weak, as the Sandinistas had few forces in the region. The MILPAS then developed rapidly in the Quilalí, Yalí and Wiwilí sectors and managed to escape the EPS because of their knowledge of the field.

MILPAS attacks were always small in scale. The first action of "Tigrillo" with 12 men was an attack on a military post in Plan de Grama defended by only three soldiers. He then attacked Santa Teresa and El Cuá first of all to obtain weapons.[36] Faced with the increase of

Combatants of the FDN proudly showing their weapons and equipment. Notable is the wide diversity of their fatigues and armament ranging from M1 Garand rifles to various other assault rifles and machine guns, and the omni-present RPG-7s. (Albert Grandolini Collection)

A platoon of well-armed and equipped *Counterrevolutionaries* (soon to become colloquially known as the 'Contras') of the FDN, armed with Kalashnikov assault rifles and PKS machine guns. (Albert Grandolini Collection)

Sandinista forces in the region, González wanted to return to Honduras for help, but he was killed in September 1980. This death disrupted the MILPAS movement that some members returned to Honduras. Those who remained in Nicaragua were poorly armed and could only conduct small skirmishes against the EPS.[37] In 1981, however, the MILPAS brought together between 2,000 and 3,000 combatants, not to mention sympathizers who could be mobilized when weapons were available. They could also rely on many supporters in the population.[38]

The Meeting of ex-GN and Campesinos

In 1980-1981, armed opposition to the Sandinistas did not appear to be a danger to the government. The FDN was indeed only a small organization with no connection to the Nicaraguan population, while farmers in the central regions were too poorly equipped to be effective.

The FDN suffered from its recruitment, which was mainly made up of former GNs who still maintain an unfavourable reputation. This poor image was maintained by the first actions carried out in Nicaragua. Operating in small groups, the ex-GN tried to gain credibility among the local population by killing undesirables in the villages, especially Sandinista officials. Civilians were also victims of crimes: murder, torture, mutilation, and rape were means used by the Contras to rally people through terror.[39] The ex-GN Pedro Pablo Ortiz Centeno "Suicida" was known in the northern part of the department of Nueva Segovia for his ill-treatment of civilians.[40]

The MILPAS, many of whose fighters and leaders were former Sandinista guerrillas, were suspicious of the ex-GN. But faced with the increasing firepower of the EPS, they were largely disadvantaged and approached the FDN in order to obtain modern weapons supplied by the Argentinians and US. In mid-1981, the MILPAS formations of "Tigrillo", Irene Calderon and Oscar Sobalvarro Garcia met in Honduras to form the Ariel base.[41] At the end of this year, the majority of MILPAS leaders returned to Honduras to be in Camp Pino 1. The FDN also sent teams to Nicaragua to rally groups of MILPAS. The latter then joined the base at La Lodosa to receive training by ex-GNs or Argentines.[42] This integration of the MILPAS into the FDN allowed the development of armed groups within Nicaragua. While at the end of 1980 they were still few in number, in the autumn of 1981 they multiplied.[43]

The merger between the FDN and the insurgent peasants of the MILPAS gave the Contras the composition they would maintain until the end of the war, i.e. a framework and a command dominated by the ex-GN, while the mass of combatants were peasants from the central regions. According to Luis Moreno, "Mike Lima", at the base at La Lodosa in the summer of 1982, only 22 of the 117 fighters were ex-GN and seven were EPS deserters, the others were peasants and in 1987, about 97% of the Contras were farmers in mountainous regions.[44]

The number of FDN personnel jumped with the arrival of the MILPAS. From 241 fighters in 1981, the FDN had about 8,000 in 1983.[45] Insurgent farmers also provided an area for the FDN in the central and northern highlands of the country. In these, a whole network of clandestine committees was formed to support the fighting units. These committees had multiple functions. They provided intelligence, found safe houses and weapons caches, helped isolated combatants reaching Honduras, provided logistics and supplies, organized alert systems around Contra units and recruited new fighters.[46]

The members of these committees, called *correos*, were unarmed but played an essential role in supporting the local Contra units as well as those crossing their areas. Often, they later became fighters. There was one correo leader per *comarca* and the correo leaders coordinated with the Contra forces in their areas.[47] According to the FDN, there was a ratio of 2.5 fighters to one correo, which represented for a total of 17,000 Contra fighters during the war from 6,000 to 7,000 correos.[48]

These support networks covered a large part of Nicaragua from Nueva Segovia to Nueva Guinea.

In early 1982, the FDN began to put in place the military structures that would remain almost unchanged until the end of the conflict. The FDN units were organized into detachments of about 20 combatants. Three detachments formed a tactical group. A *Fuerza de Tarea* or Task Force consisted of three to five tactical groups and became the main formation of the FDN.[49] Task Forces operating in the same region were grouped into a *Comando Regional* (Regional Command or CR). At the beginning of 1984, the Diriangen Task Force, which had nearly 2,000 combatants, became a CR comprising six Task Forces.[50] Over the years, the CR *Diriangen, Rafaela Herrera, Segovia, San Jacinto, Jorge Salazar 1, 2* and *3, Jose Dolores Estrada* and *Rigoberto Cabezas* were organized. At the end of the conflict there were 26 CRs leading about 100 Task Forces. In addition to these units, there was also a *Comando de Operaciones Tacticas* (FDN Special Forces), the *Fuerza Aerea* (Air Force), a Center for Military Instruction, and a Logistics Section.[51]

The complex was led by a Strategic Headquarters. Its main role was to organize logistics, communications, medical services, bases in Honduras, intelligence and coordination of military operations. It did not provide traditional hierarchical authority; decision-making power rested with regional commanders. Unit commanders, on the other hand, were most often appointed by their men. In turn, the latter selected the Task Force commanders who designated the regional commanders who, in turn, formed a Commanders' Council with supreme authority.[52]

The FDN was also beginning to develop a doctrine. As soon as it was formed, it justified its fight by its desire to establish a democratic government and restore freedom of religion and the press, and the right to private property. It was therefore strongly imbued with religion and wanted to be the defender of Nicaragua's Christian identity. The FDN thus presented itself as a democratic and Christian guerrilla group leading a crusade against Marxist and atheist Sandinistas but also as the defender of a small-owner capitalism beset by a collectivist ideology coming from the outside.[53] The propaganda on the need to restore personal freedoms met the tradition of the independence of the peasants in the central regions who formed the bulk of his troops. This speech also responded to Washington's desire to finance a "democratic" military force that would help to reduce communism in Latin America.

In early 1982, the Contras gradually emerged as an alternative political and military force to the Sandinista regime. By taking the path of armed struggle, they set themselves the objective of militarily defeating the EPS to allow the establishment of a liberal regime similar to Guatemala or Honduras.

4
THE UNDECLARED WAR OF THE REAGAN ADMINISTRATION (1981-1982)

Since 1980, the Contra forces had made only a few incursions into Nicaragua and with little success. Things changed radically when Washington, as part of its low-intensity war strategy, decided to massively support the Sandinista government's opponents.

US Policy Towards Sandinista Nicaragua

Reagan showed himself to be a supporter of a firm attitude towards the Sandinistas from the very beginning of his presidential election campaign. He violently denounced Nicaragua as a Soviet bridgehead on the American continent.[1] Managua's doctrinal proximity to the USSR and its increased dependence on the Soviets and Cubans perpetuated Reagan's anti-Sandinism. Nevertheless, he was more moderate when he came to power. First he tried to find a modus vivendi with the Sandinistas. In August 1981, Assistant Secretary of State Thomas Enders flew to Managua. He proposed that the Sandinistas stop providing guerrilla aid to El Salvador in exchange for Washington's support for the anti-Sandinista opposition being abandoned. The FSLN rejected this proposal.[2]

In February 1981, the Reagan administration, with the Covert Action Proposal for Central America, adopted a doctrine of action against the Sandinistas. The aim was to wage war on various fronts: clandestine military operations, support for military operations by opponents of Sandinism, economic destabilization in Nicaragua, a media offensive and support for social sectors opposed to the Sandinista project.[3]

The economic component of this plan was put into action in 1981 when the Reagan administration suspended $15 million in aid and refused to sell $9 million worth of wheat to Nicaragua.[4] The Inter-American Bank and the World Bank, where Washington had a dominant influence, were also blocking $390 million for social and productive projects. The Reagan administration pressured the European Union not to include Nicaragua in its aid programme for Central America, but the Europeans were not giving in. These measures were reinforced by the decision of Guatemala, Panama, Honduras, Costa Rica and El Salvador to terminate their trade relations with Nicaragua. In 1983, the sugar quota sold by Managua and guaranteed by the United States was cancelled.[5] The US strategy was clever because without foreign currency inflowing Nicaragua could no longer pay for oil from Mexico, Iran or Venezuela, its main suppliers. It could no longer sell sugar and coffee to buy food or basic necessities. Washington hoped that this would undermine popular support for the FSLN. The last stage of this economic war was the total trade embargo put in place in 1985.

In order to prevent Sandinista contagion in Central America, the United States was paying particular attention to Honduras. The US presence in the country continued to increase throughout the 1980s as Washington's aid to Tegucigalpa increased from $31 million in 1982, to $37 million in 1983, $77 million in 1984 and $88 million in 1986.[6] Honduras' military infrastructure was expanded and modernized, while roads were built or renovated near the border with Nicaragua. The Sandinista press largely echoed the US involvement in Honduras, as well as the arrival of Green Berets near the border.[7]

Since 1981, major military exercises had also been organized by the US Army and the *Fuerzas armadas de Honduras* (Honduran Armed Forces or FAR) on Honduran territory. The objective was to show the US determination to avoid revolutionary contagion in the region

The CIA not only remained in touch with survivors of the Somoza dictatorship in exile, but was quick to establish ties to a growing number of Nicaraguans that fled the country for diverse reasons in the early 1980s. This photograph shows at least three officers of the notorious US intelligence agency, with several Contras, in front of one of the Bell UH-1H Huey helicopters provided by Washington to Honduras during the early and mid-1980s. (Albert Grandolini Collection)

August 1983 and February 1984, US forces carried out *Big Pine II*, a considerably more extensive military exercise than the earlier *Big Pine* manoeuvres, involving up to 5,000 US military personnel. Extensive naval manoeuvres involved two US Navy aircraft carrier task forces, another task force led by the battleship USS *New Jersey* (BB-63) aircraft carrier and USS *Ranger* (CV-61), and a landing by the US Marines on the Caribbean coast during portions of the exercises.[9]

A simulated defence of Honduras from a mock Nicaraguan invasion was staged between February and May 1985. Called *Big Pine III* and *Universal Trek*, the military exercises involved thirty-nine US warships, as well as 7,000 US troops and 5,000 Honduran troops.[10] An even bigger show of force occurred in Honduras during Operation *Solid Shield* in May 1987. This exercise simulated a US response to a request from Honduras to help fight a Nicaraguan invasion. The Honduran phase of this operation involved more than 7,000 US military personnel as well as 3,000 Honduran soldiers.[11]

The US Navy warships and aircraft, as well as US Air Force aircraft were engaged in regular reconnaissance around, over and inside the Nicaraguan borders and airspace. The USAF and the Army Security Agency (ASA) stepped up their intelligence-gathering efforts through 1982. The Boeing RC-135s of the 55th SRW, and Boeing E-3A Sentries of the 552nd AWCW, with the support of Boeing KC-135 tankers, are known to have operated along the Nicaraguan coasts, coming from Howard AFB in Panama. The Lockheed SR-71s and U-2Rs flew directly from Beale AFB, feeding the fears of an US military intervention in Nicaragua.[12]

In November 1984, when Washington thought that Moscow was delivering MiG-21 jets to Managua, a USN task force of some 25 vessels, including the battleship USS *Iowa*, was on amphibious manoeuvres near Roosevelt Roads in Puerto Rico, in addition to which the task force with the aircraft carrier USS *Nimitz* was underway in the same direction. This was sufficient to cause the Sandinistas to mobilise 20,000 students and give them military training instead of sending them to help harvest the coffee crop: up to 25% of the crop remained unharvested, causing additional damage to the already wakened economy.

Washington was aware that economic pressures and the deployment of force in Honduras were not enough to overthrow the Sandinistas. It also knew that after the trauma of the Vietnam War, it was no longer possible for US troops to intervene directly abroad.[13] Its policy had to therefore make it possible to destabilize the Sandinista government without having to invade the country and to do so by relying on troops "by proxy." The Reagan administration's decision to strongly support the Contras was in line with this logic.

The CIA had been in contact with the *Légion 15th Septembre*. On the spot, the Agency's team, led by Duane Clarridge, coordinated the formation of the Contra forces with the help of Hondurans and Argentines. This cooperation took on a new dimension in December

The mobilisation and military training certainly provided some distraction of these two students, in November 1984, but severely disrupted the coffee harvest and thus the Nicaraguan economy. (Albert Grandolini Collection)

but above all to put pressure on Nicaragua by forcing it to divert an ever-increasing proportion of its economic and human resources to the military sector, thus weakening its economy and social stability. These manoeuvres took on a greater scale in 1983 with the *Big Pine* military exercise, which involved 4,000 Honduran soldiers and 1,600 US soldiers, as well as two landing ships and two landing craft.[8] A number of training personnel, mostly from the US Army, remained in the country to train the Honduran army in infantry tactics. Between

1981 when Reagan signed National Security Decision Directive No. 17, which authorized the CIA to conduct clandestine operations against Nicaragua in order to destabilize the Sandinistas and cut off the supply of weapons to the Salvadoran guerrillas.[14] The CIA asked for the possibility of creating a force of 500 Cuban and Nicaraguan fighters trained by the US in Honduras. It also called for secret assistance to be given to the paramilitary force formed by the former GNs with the support of Argentina. In December, Congress agreed to provide them with $20 million in assistance.

Honduras was the heart of the US operation to support the Contras. The latter's camps were located on its territory just across the border with Nicaragua from where they launched raids or mortar fire on the villages around Jalapa and Teotecacinte.[15] In Honduras, US aid arrived at Toncontín airport near Tegucigalpa, transported by C-130 Hercules aircraft.[16] There were a dozen US Army Green Berets on site to train the Contra troops while the officers were sent to the United States for training.[17] The person in charge of this support infrastructure was none other than the US ambassador in Tegucigalpa, John Negroponte who was Nixon's adviser for Vietnam assisted by the head of the local CIA station, Donald H Winter who was replaced in 1984 by Jim Adkins.[18]

US aid to the Contras continued to increase in the following years. In December 1982, it was increased to $30 million and in 1984 it was $24 million. This aid was also human, with the dispatch of military advisers, a supply of weapons and, above all, political support at the international level. Reagan said of the Contras, legitimizing their struggle: "These freedom fighters are our brothers and we must help them… They are the moral equivalent of our Founding Fathers and the brave men and women of the French Resistance."[19]

Thanks to US aid, the Contras were becoming an increasingly serious military threat to the Sandinistas. This support was fragile however, since it was regularly subject to the control of Congress, which was both sensitive to public opinion reactions and no longer wanted to give the presidency complete carte blanche, as it did in the days of Johnson and Nixon. This was what happened with the withdrawal of the Argentinians in 1982, which pushed the US to intervene directly without the presence of intermediary groups to conceal Washington's role, which went beyond the operation described by the Administration in December 1981 and voted for by Congress.[20] This provoked the latter's anger. A compromise was nevertheless reached and $19 million was finally granted to the Contras, but these funds were subject to the Boland Amendment adopted in December 1982, which prohibited the CIA from spending them to overthrow the Managua regime.[21] Despite these restrictions, in September 1983, Reagan asked the CIA to continue its clandestine operations in support of the Contras.[22]

In addition to material and military aid, the CIA also sought to build a political opposition movement acceptable both to Congress and to the public who were wary of the FDN and its image of being nostalgic for the Somoza dictatorship. The Agency became interested in a new anti-Sandinista formation that it hoped would be closer to the FDN to bring out a moderate opposition, a formation whose leader was a hero of the Sandinista revolution, Eden Pastora.

Even Eden Pastora (centre) – perhaps the most famous hero of the armed uprising against Somoza – left Nicaragua in 1981 and soon re-started the armed struggle through establishing the ARDE. He remained best-known by his famous nom de guerrre, '*Commandante* Cero' ('Commander Zero'). (Albert Grandolini Collection)

The Birth of the Southern Front

Pastora's fame, represented as a romantic and victorious guerrilla in the fight against Somoza, was initially a godsend for the FSLN. But as the Sandinistas took control of power, Pastora was gradually marginalized, certainly because of his conservative origins, which distinguished him from other Sandinista leaders. Finally, he resigned from his governmental functions in July 1981 and then officially broke with Managua on 15 April 1982.

He founded the *Alianza Revolucionaria Democratica* (ARDE) on 24 September 1982 in San Jose, Costa Rica to bring together the disappointed Sandinistas. This organization brought together different groups: the *Frente Revolucionario Sandino* (Sandino Revolutionary Front) of Pastora, the MDN of Alfonso Robelo, former member of the JGRN, the UDN-FARN of Fernando Chamorroand, and the MISURATA of Brooklyn Rivera.[23]

ARDE set up its guerrilla force in the south of Nicaragua with the support of Costa Rica, which authorized it to operate on its territory.[24] At that time, there were only 400 poorly armed fighters, most of them former Sandinistas from conservative circles but also peasants from Nueva Guinea region.[25] ARDE members did not reject the FSLN from which most of them came, but wanted to see a change in its policy so that it returned to the initial project of the anti-Somoza coalition, i.e. political pluralism, democracy, a mixed economy and non-alignment in international politics.[26] They therefore refused to allow the fight against Managua to be led by the former GN and refused the term Contras, because they believed they were still revolutionaries.[27]

Soon, Duane Clarridge, head of the CIA's Directorate of Operations for Latin America, came into contact with Pastora, whose social-democratic image could serve as a counterweight to that of the former

GNs. While ARDE called for the return of democracy, freedom of religion and the press, it refused to integrate into the East-West conflict. Pastora intended to be Sandino's heir, an image of a form of progressive nationalism concerned with national independence.

Growth in Contra Military Activity

US support for the various Contra forces was quickly making its effects felt. The ARDE increased its strength to about 2,000 fighters and benefited from modern means of communication, LAW rocket launchers, 82mm mortars, FALs, and Chinese-made AKs. With help from many US private sources, ARDE was able to establish its own "air force", led by a young Nicaraguan named Mariano, and initially equipped with two Hughes 500 helicopters. The purchase of such equipment was largely financed from $600,000 received from a former Nicaraguan ambassador to Washington, Francisco Fiallos Navarro, who lifted the funds from the embassy before defecting in 1982. A number of light transport aircraft were added later on, all flown by US mercenaries. Most of the US mercenaries contracted for ARDE were veterans of the Vietnam War and possessed considerable operational experience. Several retired higher-ranking US Army officers – including a former Lieutenant Colonel – purchased various plantations along the border between Costa Rica and Nicaragua, where small strips were cleared from which helicopters and light transport aircraft could be operated.

For the MISURA Miskitos, the first US supplies involved equipping the troops with mortars, grenade launchers, and FN FAL, and M16 rifles.[28] These units were also handled by US military advisors. The MISURA fighters were then reorganized into Task Forces with the objective of establishing themselves and attacking poorly defended Sandinista positions.[29] If the CIA provided assistance to the Miskitos and ARDE, Washington's main support was for the FDN. It then mainly consisted of Belgian-made FAL automatic rifles offered by the Honduran army, before the CIA supplied AK-47s in 1983. The US then provided M16 rifles, M79 grenade launchers, mortars, and machine guns. In October 1982, the town of San Pedro de Potrero Grande, in the department of Chinandega, was bombarded with 21 US-made mortars.[30] The modern armaments provided by Washington and the support of US military advisers enabled the Contras to carry out actions of greater scope. The strategy they adopted was largely inspired by the US who wanted to use them to hit Nicaragua's economic infrastructure and increase the fragility of its economy. It was also seeking to develop a guerrilla war based on popular support in north-central Nicaragua.

In 1981, the first units of the FDN lead only hit and run raids targeting Sandinista officials and also coffee plantations where many volunteers worked.[31] However, the need to move beyond this stage of an incursion war was gradually emerging to conduct in-depth operations and maintain a presence in the country. In January and February 1982, FDN succeeded in infiltrating 2,000 fighters into the north of the country. They achieved their first success on 14 March when a sabotage team led by José Efrén Mondragón managed to use C-4 explosives to destroy a bridge over the Rio Negro, near Somotillo, and another bridge on the Rio Coco, near Ocotal, in the department of Jinotega; both of these bridges were on one of the two main roads that lead to Honduras.[32] The sabotage unit was formed by the CIA and trained in Lepaterique near Tegucigalpa.

Operations against the bridges were followed in April 1982 by an offensive against the garrisons of border guards, particularly in Zacatera, Zacatón, La Pampas and San Francisco del Norte. In these operations FDN units from bases Pino 1, Ariel, Zebra and Nicarao, were involved, armed with AK-47 and Vz 52 rifles.[33] Other units infiltrated Nicaragua, particularly to recruit new fighters. Luis Moreno recounted one of his undercover missions that began on 27 June 1982 at the head of five detachments with a total of 14 ex-GN and 44 MILPAS. They crossed the Rio Coco near Somotine to enter the department of Jinotega. In the area of La Colonia, Moreno's troop was joined by six MILPAS fighters. But the Contras were pursued by two EPS companies of 40 men each. Finally, the Contras ambushed one of the companies, which lost nine soldiers. Thereafter, Moreno dispersed his men in four groups to recruit MILPAS fighters. Soon, he had 180 new fighters at his disposal, including Irene Calderón, a former captain of the EPS. At the beginning of August 1982, they crossed the Rio Coco to Honduras. The new recruits were then sent to a camp in Guaimaca for training.[34]

In the Atlantic region, MISURA forces were being sent to paralyse mining activity in the Bonanza and Rosita area or forestry companies north of Puerto Cabezas. Others were responsible for ambushing military convoys, attacking military posts at the border and in the coastal area as far south as Puerto Cabezas, and finally harassing the headquarters of the EPS in La Tronquera. According to the authorities, about 900 Miskitos Contras were scattered in different camps in the northern Atlantic region.[35] In September 1982, the EPS discovered two MISURA camps 60km

In 1982 and 1983, Washington's primary concern was checking the flow of arms and supplies to Nicaragua, and from there into El Salvador. On 10 October 1983, oil storage tanks in the port of Corinto were attacked by the Contras from the sea and a high proportion of Nicaragua's oil reserves were destroyed. A few days later, the oil pipeline at Puerto Sandino was also sabotaged. (Albert Grandolini Collection)

south of Puerto Cabezas.[36]

Attacks on border military posts, such as those at Leimus, Waspam or Bilwascarma, and also on Walpasiksa, Seven Benk, Bismuna and Prinzapolka were successful. In early 1983, during the attack on Bismuna in the far northwest of the country, Miskito rebels were supported by a helicopter that evacuated the wounded.[37]

The Contra incursions developed throughout 1982, sometimes over long periods, such as the one Moreno led in the autumn of 1982. The detachments he commanded were each equipped with an M79 grenade launcher, a 60mm mortar and an M60 machine gun. The mission was to support "Tigrillo", whose base, in Wina where there were about 250 volunteers, was under attack by the EPS. FDN soldiers crossed the Rio Coco and Moreno, gathered 75 men, and attacked the EPS base at Bocas de Ayapal on the Rio Bocay on 15 October. It was a success and the Contras quickly withdrew. Moreno then moved south to Caño de la Cruz where he faced an EPS patrol. He then went to El Cuá and on 22 November, he seized four government trucks and a Toyota Land Cruiser. Finally he found "Tigrillo", who led 170 fighters and more than 200 volunteers, before returning together to Honduras.[38] Through these operations, throughout 1982, the FDN evolved into a force of about 4,000 well-trained and equipped men, and 6,000 a year later.

The Contra units that infiltrated the country, sometimes for many months, needed supplies to maintain their combat capability, including ammunition, medicines and batteries for radios. To carry out these replenishing operations, the FDN, with the help of the CIA which provided T-28, C-47 and Cessna O-2 aircraft, set up an air force under the direction of Colonel Juan Gómez.[39] It also formed a helicopter squadron that included Bell UH-1B and Hughes 500 helicopters.[40] The medical resources provided enabled former Colonel Matamoros to organize an FDN medical corps at the end of 1982.[41]

At the end of 1982, fighting was permanently ongoing in the north of the country, particularly in the department of Nueva Segovia. The Contra tactics in this region were simple, they organized ambushes and then withdraw to Honduras under the protection of mortars.[42]

In response to the increase in Contra activities, the JGRN declared a state of emergency in March 1982 and introduced a system of prior censorship for the press. This situation had given the authorities great powers to control or repress dissidents. *La Prensa*, the opposition newspaper, continued to be published in a highly censored manner until 1986, when it was closed but reopened only 18 months later.[43]

Training of 'Contra' recruits in Honduras in 1984. (US DoD)

The FAS hit back on 3 October 1983, when its troops used Soviet-made SA-7 missiles (see below for details) to shoot down this DC-3 used to para-drop supplies for the ARDE near Matabalpa. The crew of four was captured, and reported that their flight had originated from a CIA-base in Honduras. (Albert Grandolini Collection)

The Contra Air Force(s)

The Contra units that had infiltrated Nicaragua were often underway in complete isolation for months. They were thus in need of supplies to maintain their combat capability, including not only food, ammunition, and medicine, but also batteries for their radios. To carry out the necessary resupply operations, the ARDE operated at least seven small aircraft and one helicopter as early as of 1983, and this number grew significantly over the following years. The FDN – with help of the CIA – had set up a rival air force under the direction of Colonel Juan Gómez, but very little is known about this service, except that it was mostly staffed by Nicaraguans, including many former FAN and GN officers and other ranks.[44]

The flying services supporting the ARDE and the FDN eventually grew into two units, one flying at least 29 aircraft over this time, while the other operated various helicopters. The aircraft included one Douglas DC-6 and one Lockheed Hudson, several Douglas DC-3/C-47s, a miscellany of Cessnas (including two 337s) and Pipers, and two North American T-28s. The majority of these were based at airfields like Ilopango in El Salvador and 'the Farm' – Aguacate – in Honduras: most received a camouflage pattern in diverse shades of dark green, sometimes tan or brown, and wore no national – or any other – insignia. The DC-6 alone is known to have made over 160 airdrops by 1987. Due to the lack of advanced navigation systems, the majority of operations were undertaken along the Rio Coco – i.e. included either no, or only shallow penetrations of Nicaraguan airspace, and by daylight: when this caused the first few losses, the aircrews began flying at altitudes above 3,650m (12,000ft), to remain outside the reach of SA-7s, thus decreasing the precision of their airdrops. Indeed, numerous firefights between the EPS and the FDN erupted while one or the other side attempted to collect the supplies deployed by aircraft.

The 'helicopter squadron' of the FDN's air force included at least two Bell UH-1Bs (reports about UH-1Hs remain unconfirmed), one Bell 206 Jet Ranger, two Hughes 365s or OH-6As, and two Hughes 500s. Like the transports, these were foremost flown by Nicaraguan personnel (although frequently serviced by the US mercenary technical personnel), mostly painted in dark green, and wore no, or only a bare minimum of any kind of insignia.[45]

Finally, the US Army provided some of its helicopters to support the Contras, time and again. For example, on 11 January 1984, a Bell OH-58 Kiowa (military variant of the Bell 206 Jet Ranger) of the US Army was shot down near the border between Nicaragua and Honduras: the pilot was shot in the exchange of fire with the EPS, while two sabotage-experts managed to run away. Less than two months later, a UH-1H of the US Army carrying US Senators J. Bennet Johnson and Lawton Chiles, and six crew members, took fire while underway near Colomoncagua. Before the pilot was able to fly away, one bullet destroyed the radio, while another tore through the floor and exited through the roof, narrowly missing Chiles and clipping one of the rotor blades. Around the same time, the crew of a Bell AH-1 Huey Cobra helicopter gunship of the US Army also reported coming under attack 'from a MiG warplane of unknown nationality'.[46]

Other aircraft involved in supporting the Contras included two Grumman OV-1D reconnaissance aircraft of the 224th Military Intelligence Battalion of the US Army, and also Cessna A-37B and UH-1Hs of the Honduran Air Force. In September 1985, two Dassault Super Mystére B.2 fighter-bombers of the same service (both modified to the 'Sa'ar' standard in Israel before their re-export to the Central American nation, and armed with Israeli-made Shafrir Mk.II air-to-air missiles in addition to 30mm DEFA

A rare view of one of the CIA-operated forward helicopter bases near the Rio Coco on the border between Honduras and Nicaragua. The ground crew is busy unloading supplies from the UH-1B on the ground, while the Hughes 500 provides top cover. (Albert Grandolini Collection)

One of at least two Cessna 337s operated by the CIA on behalf of the ARDE and FDN. While one of the two aircraft is known to have received a disruptive camouflage pattern in dark green and dark brown, this example was left in light grey overall, and seems to have carried an unknown civilian registration. Notably, it was never armed: the FAS retained aerial superiority in the Nicaraguan skies for the duration of the conflict. (Albert Grandolini Collection)

NICARAGUA, 1961–1990, VOLUME 2: THE CONTRA WAR

The 'Cuzco' was a do-it-yourself armoured car, consisting of a superstructure made of simple metal plates, welded atop the chassis of a commercial car. As far as is known, it remained a one-off: reportedly, it had already survived lots of action during the final days of the war against the Somoza regime, and then into the Contra War. (Artwork by David Bocquelet)

The BTR-60PBs of the sole Mechanised Infantry Battalion of the EPS retained their olive green overall colour, applied before delivery, but received big, three-digit turret numbers, apparently indicating their assignment to a specific company. (Artwork by David Bocquelet)

The most powerful armoured fighting vehicle of the Contra War was the Soviet-made T-55 main battle tank. Nicaragua acquired a total of 110, and these became the primary armament of a total of five armoured battalions of the EPS, each of which operated 22. As far as is known, all retained their olive green overall colour, but usually received big three-digit turret numbers, possibly also unit markings. Ironically, because the leadership in Managua was seriously concerned about the possibility of a US invasion, the five units saw very little action against the Contras: instead, they were held in strategic reserve. (Artwork by David Bocquelet)

i

The wave of defections that followed the fall of the Somoza regime, and the poor economic situation reduced the fleet of aircraft taken over by the FAS to a bare minimum. Only three Cessna 337s are known to have been available as of the 1979-1981 period: the number seemingly decreased to two (serial numbers 152 and 153) for most of the Contra War. The few available photographs from the 1980s show them wearing a disruptive camouflage pattern in tan (or light green) and dark green as shown here, and armed with US- or French-made pods for 68mm unguided rockets. This example is shown with original FAS insignia applied on the fin: from around 1981, at least by 1984, this was replaced by the Nicaraguan tricolore. (Artwork by Tom Cooper)

The number of AT-33As operated by the FAS was also limited to three, of which two were operational on average. Between 1979 and the mid-1980s – when they were withdrawn from service – the aircraft were partially re-painted at least twice, resulting in a very colourful camouflage pattern as illustrated here: the original light grey overall was enhanced with tan and dark green, and then with additional tan and black. Like Cessna 337s, they originally wore the FAS national insignia on the fin, but by the mid-1980s this was replaced with the Nicaraguan tricolore, and a roundel applied on the rear fuselage. (Artwork by Tom Cooper)

In 1980, Nicaragua acquired two UH-1Cs from private sources in the USA. Both received a camouflage pattern in tan and dark green (and had their undersurfaces pained in light grey), applied directly over their original olive drab overall. Both were soon out of service: one crashed under unknown circumstances, while the other had to be abandoned for the lack of spares. Nevertheless, they are known to have received at least a fin flash and the service title in black on the boom. The sole known serial number is shown here: 260. (Artwork by Tom Cooper)

NICARAGUA, 1961–1990, VOLUME 2: THE CONTRA WAR

The six SF.260Ws donated to Nicaragua by Libya are known to have retained their original camouflage pattern consisting of light sand, dark beige and olive green on upper surfaces and sides, and light admiralty grey on undersurfaces. Most seem to have had their wing-tip fuel tanks painted in white. Libyan SF.260s used to wear national markings in the form of green roundels in six positions, and a 'fin flash' in green: while their roundels were overpainted or removed without replacement, the Nicaraguans added their own serials (apparently with a 'shadow' in red) and their tricolore on the fin. This example is shown equipped with an additional drop tank on the underwing hardpoint. (Artwork by Tom Cooper)

The 14 Mi-8TBRs delivered to Nicaragua between 1981 and 1984 were colloquially known as Mi-8Ts. It seems that each wore an entirely different camouflage pattern: indeed, some wore civilian markings of the Soviet airline Aeroflot on their arrival. This example was camouflaged in beige (BS381C/388) and blue-green on top surfaces and sides, and light admiralty grey (BS381C/697) on undersurfaces. Their serials were always applied in black below the cockpit, and repeated at the bottom of the fin, underneath the fin flash. Armament consisted of UB-16-57 rocket pods and a 12.7mm machine gun installed in the nose. (Artwork by Tom Cooper)

At least two, possibly more of the early Nicaraguan Mi-17s arrived wearing this camouflage in beige and dark earth (BS381C/350) or dark brown (BS381C/411) on upper surfaces and sides, and light admiralty grey (BS381C/697) on undersurfaces. As on Mi-8Ts, national markings consisted of a big roundel on the rear of the cabin, and a fin flash. Serial numbers were applied in black on the armour plate below the cockpit and the bottom of the fin: note that several of the early Mi-17s had received the serials of Mi-8Ts written off early after arrival in Nicaragua. Usual armament consisted of either two or four UB-32-57 rocket pods and up to two UPK-23 gun pods. (Artwork by Tom Cooper)

iii

The final batch of Mi-17s – which reached Nicaragua in 1986 – was manufactured to the Mi-8MTV-2 standard and included big box-like exhaust diffusers to lessen their vulnerability to MANPADs. Most were originally painted in grey-green (BS381C/283) and either olive drab (BS381C/298) or dark green (BS381C/641) on upper surfaces and sides: the lighter colour tended to bleach into a shade similar to beige. Undersurfaces were painted in light admiralty grey (BS381C/697), and all received the usual set of national markings and serial numbers. Gauging by the available photographs and videos, their usual armament consisted of four UB-32-57 rocket pods, and the nose-mounted 12.7mm machine gun. (Artwork by Tom Cooper)

All the Mi-25s operated by the FAS wore the same, standardised camouflage pattern applied on almost all the helicopters of this variant exported World-wide in the late 1970s and through the 1980s. While applied in slight variations, this consisted of yellow sand and green on upper surfaces and sides, and light blue on undersurfaces. Markings included a big roundel on the rear of the fuselage, the service title in black, the fin flash and the serial number (applied only on the front fuselage). Typical armament in the mi-1980s included a pair each of UB-32-57 rocket pods and UPK-23 gun pods. This helicopter survived the attack of two Honduran SMB.2s on 17 March 1988. (Artwork by Tom Cooper)

The second batch of Mi-25s (or Mi-24s, according to alternative reports) arrived in Nicaragua in 1986, already equipped with exhaust diffusers. While still painted in the same colours as the first one (applied along the same, standardised pattern), these proved to be less resistant to the local climatic conditions and rapidly bleached under the tropical sun and rain. The service title was also slightly different, and applied with more inclination. The use of MANPADs and the loss of two Mi-25s prompted the FAS crews to engage their targets from longer range, in turn reducing weapon selection to four UB-32-57 rocket pods – in addition to the 12.7mm six-barrel machine gun installed in the barbette under the chin. (Artwork by Tom Cooper)

NICARAGUA, 1961–1990, VOLUME 2: THE CONTRA WAR

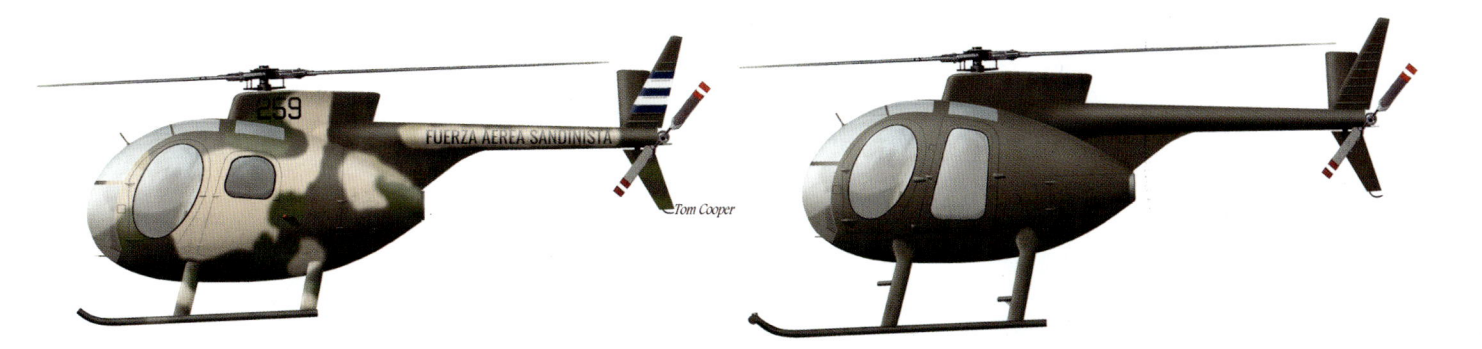

Both the FAS and the Contras flew Hughes helicopters during the Contra War. The FAS took over at least two OH-6As left over from the former FAN. A reconstruction of one (serial 259) is shown on the left side: the original olive drab colour was crudely overpainted with sand and dark green, the large service title applied on the boom, and the serial on the gear-box cowling. The Contras also flew two Huges 365 or OH-6As. US mercenaries flying for the Contras active along the border with Honduras operated at least two Huges 500s (right illustration) – of which one suffered technical problems and had to be cannibalized to provide spares for the other – in 1984: both were painted in olive drab or dark green overall. (Artworks by Tom Cooper)

A reconstruction of one of at least two UH-1Bs operated by the Contras. This example retained its olive drab overall colour, but received a personal name – 'Lady Ellen' – in white and black on the cockpit door. The majority of the aircraft and helicopters operated by the Contras – over time the fleet included several DC-3/C-47s, one Douglas DC-6 and one Lockheed Hudson, a miscellany of Cessnas (including two O-2A/FTB.337s) and Pipers, and two North American T-28s – wore no insignia at all. Flown by Nicaraguan crews from airfields like Ilopango in El Salvador and 'the Farm' (Aguacate) in Honduras, they rarely ventured anywhere deeper over Nicaragua. (Artwork by Tom Cooper)

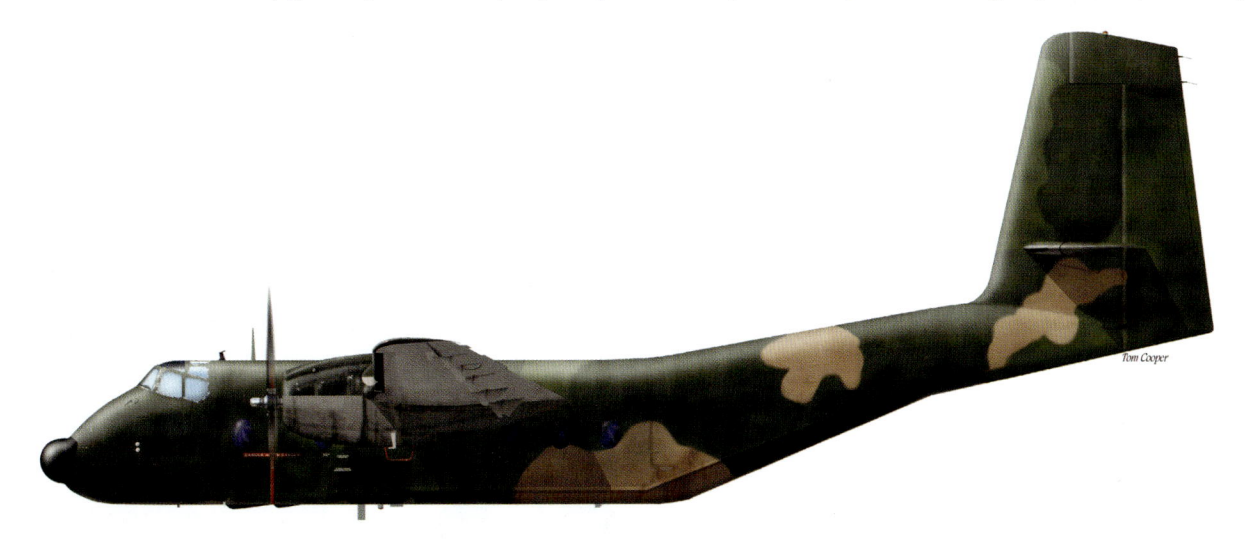

A reconstruction of one of two C-7s operated by the ACE as of 1985-1987. Led by ex-Air America-pilot William J Cooper, and ex-USAF officers Bob Dutton and Dick Gadd, this was a private venture contracted by the CIA, that mostly operated from 'the Farm'. Other than the C-123K shot down over Nicaragua, none wore any national markings and – apparently – no other markings or registrations either. Both Caribous retained their – meanwhile badly worn out, and very dirty – 'South East Asia' camouflage patterns in tan (FS30219), green (FS34102) and dark green (FS34079) on upper surfaces and sides, and light grey (FS36622) on undersurfaces. (Artwork by Tom Cooper)

v

ARDE, female guerrilla, Southern Nicaragua, 1985

While typically wearing a baseball cap, ARDE's combatants were well-equipped for combat in the Central American jungle. This young female is shown wearing a combat uniform in the BDU pattern, US-made jungle boots, and a M1961 belt with ammunition pouches in combination with items of modern All-Purpose Lightweight Individual Carrying Equipment (ALICE) gear – all of US Army origin. She is shown armed with a small knife, and an old Soviet-made AKS assault rifle. Also notable is the Sandinista scarf around her neck and a badge with the silhouette of Sandino sewn to the right shoulder; many of the ARDE were former Sandinistas and believed that they were carrying forward the spirit of the revolution. (Artwork by Anderson Subtil)

FDN, Commando de Operaciones Especiales (COE), guerrilla, Yamales Training Camp, Honduras, 1987

The FDN always sought to standardise the dress of its combatants. While never achieving this, the most usual outfit included an all-blue uniform with the sign of this organisation on the left shoulder combined with the ubiquitous jungle hat and the ALICE canvas belt. The fighter is shown while undergoing training on General Dynamics FIM-43 Red Eye MANPAD, delivered as a countermeasure against heavy deployment of armed helicpters by the Sandinistas. (Artwork by Anderson Subtil)

BLI (Battallón de Lucha Irregular), irregular infantry solider, Operation Danto 88, March 1988

Unlike conventional EPS troops – who wore a light green or light tan ensemble that was Cuban by inspiration – members of the BLIs usually wore uniforms with varying camouflage patterns. The most widespread was 'brown leaf' and (within the BLI Socrates Sandino) the old US 'duck hunter', shown here. Standard, rubber-soled boots, a Soviet tropical field hat, canvas belt, a canteen – all probably of Cuban origin – and the typical Chinese-style chest rig (from East Germany) – usually completed their gear. His typical weapon was an AKM assault rifle, here shown with a 30-rounds plastic magazine. (Artwork by Anderson Subtil)

NICARAGUA, 1961–1990, VOLUME 2: THE CONTRA WAR

One batch of Mi-17s delivered to the FAS in the 1986-1987 period included helicopters (known serials include 293 and 303) painted in rather ill-suited 'desert' camouflage pattern. Another notable detail about the example with serial number 303 – visible in this photograph – is the 'extension' of the light admiralty grey colour from the underside of the cabin high up the nose. (Albert Grandolini Collection)

One of the last Mi-17s delivered to Nicaragua was this example, serial number 333. Originally consisting of grey-green and olive green, the camouflage pattern was bleached by the local weather into two shades of grey. Nevertheless, the service title and national markings remained clearly visible. (Albert Grandolini Collection)

Major Roberto Amador used to serve with the FAN until 1979. Subsequently, he flew C-47s for the Contras until shot down by the Sandinistas in 1987. While his entire crew was killed on the ground, he managed to evade captivity. (Roberto Amador Collection, via Kike Maracas)

The first of the two UH-1Bs operated by the Contras in the mid-1980s was nick-named 'Lady Ellen': this ex-US Army helicopter retained its original olive drab overall. (Roberto Amador Collection, via Kike Maracas)

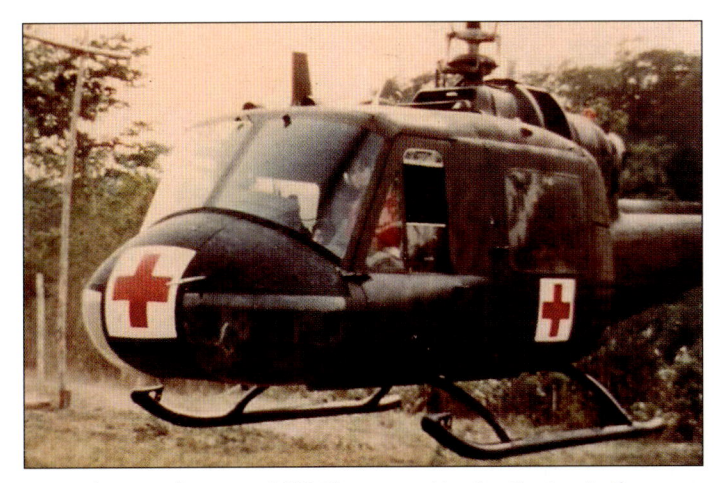

This was the second UH-1B operated by the Contras in the mid-1980s. While receiving a disruptive camouflage pattern consisting of stripes in dark green applied over the original livery in olive drab, the big red crosses around the fuselage indicated its primary purpose: casualty evacuation. (via Kike Maracas).

One of several Hughes helicopters (either a Hughes 369 or an ex-US Army OH-6A) that was operated by the Contras. This example seems to have received big splotches of green and tan atop its original colour, and might have worn a small serial number 50 applied on the front part of the boom. (via Kike Maracas)

vii

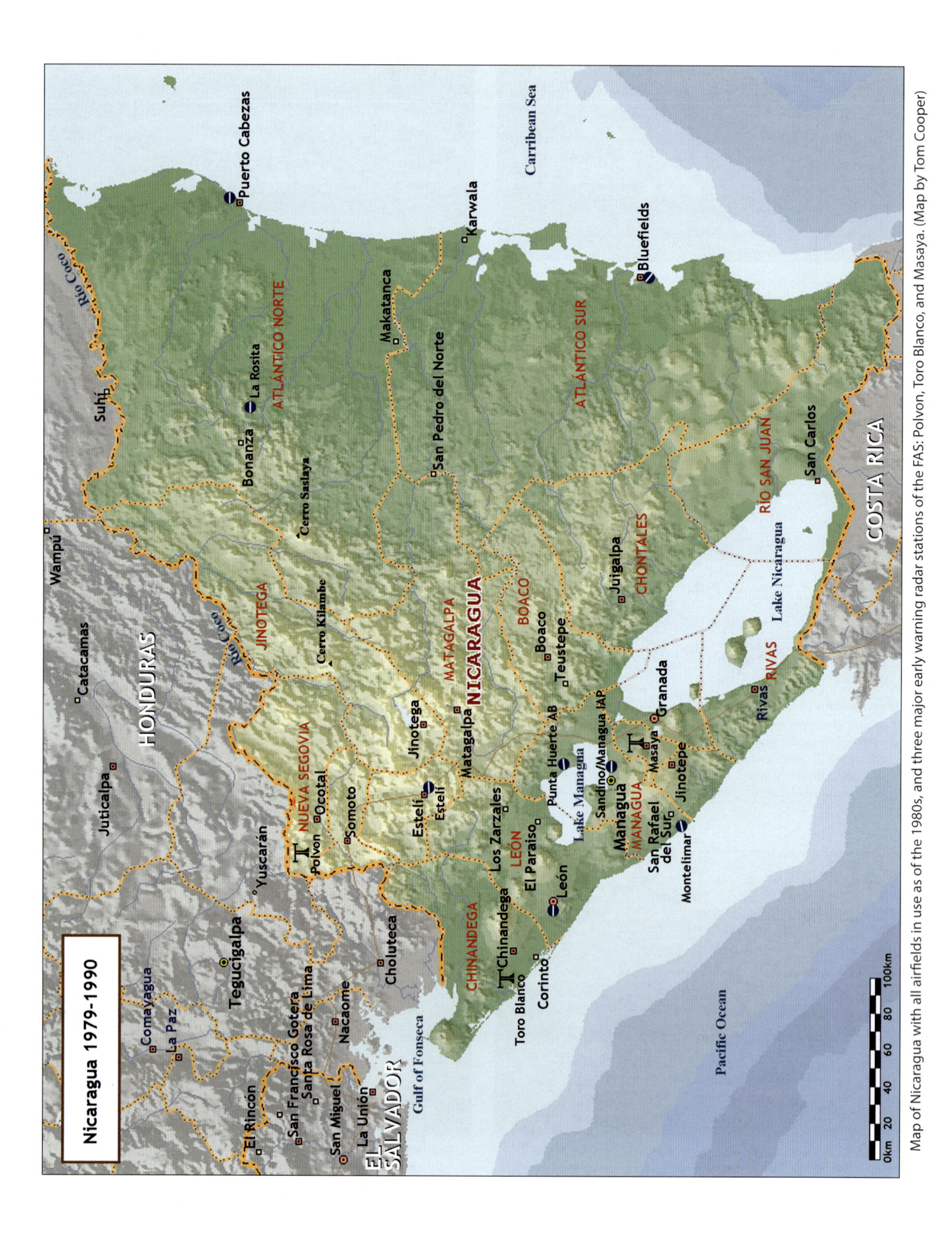

Map of Nicaragua with all airfields in use as of the 1980s, and three major early warning radar stations of the FAS: Polvon, Toro Blanco, and Masaya. (Map by Tom Cooper)

NICARAGUA, 1961–1990, VOLUME 2: THE CONTRA WAR

This was one of two C-123Ks acquired by ACE for operations in support of the ARDE. (Albert Grandolini Collection)

An AH-1 Cobra helicopter gunship of the US Army during the Exercise Golden Pheasant in 1988. What kind of a 'MiG' the crew of one of these sighted while underway near the border with Nicaragua, four years earlier, remains unknown. (Albert Grandolini Collection)

Part of the Aguacate airfield in Honduras – nicknamed 'the Farm' by its users – as seen in 1983. Visible are both of ACE's C-7 Caribous, and also the DC-6, a C-47 (foreground), and the sole Hudson operated by the Contras. (US Department of State)

Ilopango airport in El Salvador was one of two major bases from which the CIA ran aerial operations against Nicaragua in the 1980s. This clandestinely-taken photograph was taken in 1986, and shows at least three C-47/DC-3s operated on behalf of the Contras: one is visible on the left side, and two others above the roof of the main airport terminal). (Albert Grandolini Collection)

A Sikorsky UH-60 Black Hawk helicopter of the US Army rushing to aid the crew of a CIA-operated Bell 206 Jet Ranger that crashed for unknown reasons inside Honduras, near the border with Nicaragua, on 1 December 1984. (Albert Grandolini Collection)

internal cannons) entered Nicaraguan airspace to – reportedly – claim one of the FAS helicopters, too. It remains unclear if the latter was a Mi-8, Mi-17, or Mi-25.[47]

In April 1986, the CIA helped the retired Major General Richard Secord of the US Army, and former Air America employee John F Piowaty, to launch the company named Amalgamated Commercial Enterprises (ACE; also known as 'Contra Air'). During the same year, ACE recruited between 25 and 30 pilots and other crewmembers, mostly former employees of Air America (six had extensive experience from South East Asia), Continental Air Transport and Southern Air Transport. The chief pilot became William J Cooper, while further down the chain of command were Bob Dutton and Dick Gadd (both former USAF officers that had served under Secord at earlier times). ACE acquired two 'worn out' Fairchild C-123K Provider transports, two 'nearly worn-out' DHC C-7A Caribous, and an 'inappropriate', single-engine Maule MX-7. All lacked reliable radars and navigation systems, and arrived with next to no spare parts. One of the C-123s overshot the runway at one of the airstrips in northern Costa Rica, shortly after entering service: the aircraft was recovered, but subsequently ACE switched to El Salvador and Honduras instead. Lacking advanced means of navigation – but also because their 'customers' had next to no training in marking and lightning drop zones – most of ACE's operations had to be undertaken by day: the aircraft flew at critically low altitudes, frequently dodging not only ground fire, but also FAS Mi-25s. At least one of the C-123Ks is known to have brushed a tree during an evasion manoeuvre, and was subsequently written off, while the other was shot down by the EPS in September 1986.[48]

Finally, the US did offer and provide a number of boats, enabling the Contras to launch naval raids on port facilities and even some of the ships operated by the Sandinistas – sometimes supported by Honduran military aircraft – but very little is known about these.

5

GRENADA 1983 – NICARAGUA 1984

With US support for funding, armament, and training, and a solid rear base in Honduras and Costa Rica, Contra forces were able, in early 1983, to strike harder and harder at the Sandinista government. They became a real threat to the revolutionary project defended by the FSLN.

In Search of a Liberated Area

At the end of 1982, the Contras organized an offensive, *Plan C*, targeting the regions of Santa Clara, Teotecacinte and Jalapa in the department of Nueva Segovia. The objective was to establish a liberated area where the FDN could install a provisional government junta that could be recognized by Washington and its allies.[1] The operation began on 7 December 1982 when the FDN held a press conference in Florida to present its leadership, which included only civilians with the exception of Bermúdez. Adolfo Calero Portocarrero, leader of the Conservative Party and former leader of Coca-Cola in Nicaragua, was appointed Commander-in-Chief and head of the Political Directorate. By presenting a moderate face, the aim was to show to the US people the democratic and civil nature of the Contras.

About a thousand fighters led by Pedro Centeno "El Suicida", supported by 60mm, 81mm, and 106mm mortars, attacked with the objective of seizing Jalapa and Sotomo between 13 and 15 December.[2] Moreno's troops also entered Nicaragua and marched towards Las Piedras where they had to face the border guards in battle.[3] In the neighbouring Atlantic region, about 260 MISURA fighters massed in the Bismuna and El Kum area with the objective of seizing Puerta Cabezas but had to withdraw quickly from the EPS.[4]

In the Jalapa region, the EPS had only local border guard and MPS units. To repel the Contra attack, the Sandinista staff sent 14 Reserve Infantry Battalions, two Permanent Infantry Battalions, a Mechanized Infantry Battalion with BTR-60BPs, a border guard detachment and an artillery group with 152mm guns, 107mm rocket launchers, 120mm and 82mm mortars and anti-aircraft equipment.[5] The EPS suffered heavy casualties during the fighting, and Jalapa and surrounding cities were damaged, but the Contra attack was finally repelled and FDN forces were forced to retreat to Honduras. They then had nearly 9,000 combatants, most often farmers from the MILPAS.[6]

Despite the failure of the offensive on Jalapa, the FDN continued its incursions into Nicaragua. The desire to seize Jalapa and create a liberated area was not abandoned. The Siembra plan was being implemented for this purpose. Tasks Forces made deep incursions to divert the Sandinistas from the main objective, Jalapa. Thus the unit commanded by Walter Saúl Calderón López "Toño" headed for Matagalpa and Boaco in February 1983.[7] The Contras attacked many garrisons such as that of San José de las Mulas in the Matagalpa mountains. After three months of operation, pursued by EPS units, the 280 fighters were attacked in Santa Elena, Rancho Grande, Matagalpa and La Golondrina, near San José de Bocay, where they were surrounded. Nevertheless, they managed to break the encirclement and return to Honduras.[8] In March, various columns of about 1,200 men operated in the Wiwili and Quilali regions with the intention of seizing the Jalapa Valley, while others, of only a few fighters, operated within 100km of Managua.[9] To ensure the supply of troops, the Contras used an airstrip near the Rio Bocay but it was quickly destroyed by the FAS while violent fighting took place in the Cerro Chachagua near Quilali. Finally, the Contras had to withdraw.[10]

In April, clashes took place in the department

Fighting for Jalapa in December 1982 was not easy for the EPS, which suffered heavy losses while rushing reinforcements to the scene, and having these running into insurgent ambushes. This BTR-60PB of the EPS's sole Mechanised Infantry Battalion was blown over to its side. (Albert Grandolini Collection)

Evacuation of an injured Sandinista soldier with the help of one of only two SE.316B Alouette IIIs operated by the FAS. (via Kike Maracas)

of Jinotega in the sectors of San José de Bocay and Wiwili but also in the department of Chinandega.[11] That same month, two Task Forces tried to seize Jalapa in a pincer manoeuvre. They approached very close to the city but had to withdraw in the face of the resistance of the EPS. On 21 April, supported by mortars and M60 machine guns, the Contras tried to seize Cuidad Sandino, and then on 30 April about 1,200 Contras fought the EPS at Filas de la Yegua and Terrerias, 13km north of Jalapa.[12] At the end of April and beginning of May, it was in the department of Nueva Segovia that fighting took place between the Sandinistas and Contras commanded by Pedro Ortiz "El Suicida" and then against the Macarali border post defended by the border guards.[13]

At the end of May, clashes were still concentrated around Jalapa, particularly in El Porvenir.[14] In June, violent fighting took place around Jalapa and Teotecacinte, which was attacked on 3 June. The Contras seized El Porvenir, a few kilometres from the border, but they had to retreat from the assault of a thousand EPS soldiers. Nevertheless, they managed to destroy tobacco plantations and many shops. Half of the region's tobacco harvest was lost, representing about $3 million.[15] In July, fighting took place in Boca de Piedra and Buhbu in Matagalpa department, Yali in Jinotega department, north of Waslala in Nueva Segovia department, and in Consuelo in Zelaya department.[16] On 10 August, soldiers of "Tigrillo" killed 14 peasants in an ambush in El Cedro in the department of Jinotega. In the same department, fighting took place in Tawas, Los Nogales, San Juan del Norte.[17] In the second half of August, the FDN launched an offensive, attacking Ciudad Sandino, San Rafael del Norte, Los Tablones.[18]

While in the north of the country, FDN tried in vain to seize Jalapa to constitute a liberated area, in the south, ARDE forces began to take action in April 1983. They established some bases in Nicaragua to launch incursions, sometimes at long distances, reaching Nueva Guinea 70km north of the border or on the Rio Maiz where speed boats from Costa Rica landed fighters. In April 1983, the ARDE attacked the Papturro border post and launched about 20 attacks in the following two months. In May, it attacked the border posts of La Esperanza and Fatima and fought the EPS in Las Azucenas valley in the department of Rio San Juan.[19]

Three EPS battalions, about 2,400 soldiers, responded by patrolling an area of nearly 2,000km², destroying about 20 ARDE camps, one of which had a helicopter landing area.[20] Nevertheless, on 28 June, it was San Juan del Norte that was attacked by the Contras and at the end of July the border post of Peñas Blancas.[21] On 10 August, ARDE launched an offensive to reach Bluefield. Fighting took place on the Rio Maiz, on the Rio Indio and at Harry Creek. The fiercest clashes took place on the Rio Maiz where the ARDE dug trenches and installed mortars and rocket launchers. On 8 September, the EPS pushed Pastora's forces back to Costa-Rica.[22]

Change of Strategy
A 1983 CIA report noted the military failure of the Contras. Duane Clarridge therefore called for a change in the FDN's strategy and tactics that he considered too conventional in military terms. He was listened to by Bill Casey who wanted both to destroy Nicaragua's economic infrastructure and increase deep incursions into the country.[23] In July, Clarridge arrived in Tegucigalpa where he outlined the Agency's new objective for the Contras: to cut Nicaragua's oil supplies to weaken its resilience and reduce the capacity of the EPS to act. He recommended that the FDN focused on the destruction of Nicaragua's economic infrastructure. In this way, it was a question of eroding public support for the government. This new strategy had to be accompanied by the conquest of the population through armed propaganda. To do this, it was necessary to form areas within the country where Contra forces would be able to stay permanently and have logistical and operational autonomy.

The Diriangen Task Force was entrusted with the task of destroying the State farms near Condega, San Juan del Rio Coco and San Rafael del Norte, which it tried to take over in July 1983.[24] That same month a Contra fighter was arrested by the DGSE when he was attempting to sabotage a geothermal power plant in the department of Léon.[25]

The campaign against the Nicaraguan economy took a new dimension in September. At dawn on 8 September 1983, two T-28s approached Managua flying at a very low level. The first dropped

New recruits of the FDN seen while undergoing training in Honduras in 1983. (Photo by S Clevenger, via J. H.)

FAS troops mortaring positions of the Contras along the border to Honduras in June 1983. (US Department of State)

a bomb near the home of Foreign Minister Miguel D'Escoto. The bomb missed and nobody was injured: the T-28 came away without encountering any opposition, but was said to have crashed in Rio San Juan Province; the crew including Agustín Roman (a Nicaraguan who once worked for Aeronica), and Sebastián Muller (a deserter from the FAS), were killed.[26] A few minutes later, the second Trojan attacked Managua's Augusto César Sandino Airport. It roared in low over the runway and dropped a 250kg bomb on the adjacent military side, destroying four military vehicles, damaging the hangar of Aeronica (the national airline), mortally wounding one and injuring three other soldiers. The next morning, the ARDE aircraft struck again. Two T-28s rocketed the port of Corinto, hitting the local oil and chemical storage tanks – and barely missing a Soviet freighter. Other bombers attacked Sandinista troops near the Costa Rican border, and the Sandinistas claimed that one of the aircraft had been shot down.[27] Also in September, an aircraft from Costa Rica bombed a power plant in Nicarao.[28] On 3 October, two ARDE speedboats attacked the Puerto Zeledon fuel depot.[29] Two high-voltage lines near the border with Costa Rica were also destroyed.[30] In Corinto, on 10 October 1983, 25,000 people were temporarily forced to leave their homes after two speedboats stormed the port to shoot at the shore, destroying eight storage tanks containing 3.4 million gallons of oil.[31] In the same month a new attack hit Puerto Sandino where the oil pipeline was destroyed. These raids originated from the Gulf of Fonseca, and the boats carrying the saboteurs were accompanied by FAH UH-1H helicopter gunships. These operations were actually carried out by CIA agents but were claimed by the FDN or ARDE in order to keep the Agency's actions secret.

The Contra ground units were still participating in this campaign against the country's economic infrastructure. In October, the Diriangen Task Force, with 426 fighters, was near San Juan del Rio Coco, in the vicinity of Jinotega, after having crossed the RM 1 which was its main area of action.[32] It seized Pantasma on October 18, destroying economic facilities worth $3 million and killing about 100 EPS soldiers.[33] Shortly thereafter, it was in Los Condegas Valley when it was almost surrounded by 2,000 to 3,000 EPS soldiers, but managed to escape before receiving resupply by aircraft.[34] Further west in the department of Nueva Segovia, on 27 September, the Contras destroyed the border post of El Espino while a column tried to seize Ocotal and destroyed a bridge over the Rio Coco river.[35] In total, the FDN destroyed about 200 State farms in 1983.[36]

Contras Settle Inside Nicaragua

Operations against economic targets also aimed to maintain activity in the area of operation from Rio Gusanera to La Mesas de Moropotente and the Pan-American Highway near Estelí, which represented a favourable infiltration route to reach the centre of the country. The Contras' infiltrations were carried out from the base camps of the La Vegas salient in Honduras at La Lodosa base.[37] The fighters were trained in these camps before entering Nicaragua through small columns of about 20 men each. These columns were separate but nevertheless close enough to support each other in case of danger. They could gather to form a larger force, but more often they acted separately to ambush or strike economic objectives. The ability of the Contras to assemble different columns to form large combat forces quickly became a major problem for the Sandinistas.

Once inside the country, they gradually dismantled cooperatives in mountainous rural areas, recruited fighters and organized support networks of civilians to protect, supply and provide information for them. They did not conduct major military operations because they did not wish to attract EPS attention, their mission being more political than military.[38]

The Contras ventured deeper into the country. CR Jorge Salazar, led by *Commandante* Juan Ramón Riva "Quiché" left Honduras and settled permanently in the Zelaya area, east of the RM 6. Recruitment among farmers allowed them to form five additional command groups all led by peasants.[39] Meanwhile, other units advanced in the Matagalpa department. It was during these deep incursions that the FDN operated one of the first air resupply operations with a C-47 on 18 September 1983.[40] As the operations intensified in duration and scope, the Contras began using helicopters (including a few UH-1Bs) and transport aircraft for dropping supplies to their fighters underway inside Nicaragua. These operations, organized by Colonel Céspedes, were not without risk since a C-47 was shot down by the Sandinista anti-aircraft troops on 3 October 1983 in the Matagalpa department.

Gradually, throughout 1983, the military forces of the Contras infiltrated more and more deeply with the objective of establishing control over geographical areas that correspond to the areas of operations entrusted to each CR. In these areas, the FDN received support from part of the peasantry, which allowed it to easily move its troops across a very wide range of territories from the Honduran border to San José de Bocay, El Rosario and Wamblan, El Cuá, Wiwili, Rio Tuma, Dalia, Rio Blanco, to the east of Matiguas, San Pedro del Norte, Bocana de Paiwas, east of Boaco, El Ayote, El Tortuguero, Wapi and Chontales, El Rama, Nueva Guinea to the San Juan River which forms the border with Costa Rica.[41]

These Contra infiltrations compelled Humberto Ortega to recognize that the military situation was becoming "difficult" for the EPS. However, the majority of Contra attacks during

A truck full of EPS regulars rushing towards another combat zone in late 1983. (Albert Grandolini Collection)

this period occurred mainly in the Atlantic region and, according to the government, they sought to seize Puerto Cabezas. But MISURA's actions in the coastal area had poor results, while operations in the mining area turned into a fiasco and some, such as the attempt to take the Tronquera in August 1983, were a disaster.[42] ARDE groups also made incursions into the south from Costa Rica.[43] In September, they attacked the town of Peñas Blancas destroying customs facilities, while two aircraft bombarded the El Naranjo area.[44]

In September 1983, the FDN launched Operation *Marathon*, which aimed to take over Ocotal. The forces led by Commander Benito Bravo "Mack" and former Colonel Echeverry "Fierro" tried to seize the city, but this frontal attack was another failure.[45] In October, Clarridge again asked the FDN to launch a new major offensive to "liberate" a small part of Nicaraguan territory and installed a Junta of government there. From this territory, Contra forces would be able to infiltrate and settle permanently in the heart of the country. The objective of the Sierra Plan, as in 1982, aimed for the Jalapa region. But the EPS resisted the attack and, as in the previous year, the FDN Contras had to retreat and take refuge in Honduras.[46]

The Contra Pressure Increased

In 1984, the Contras continued to pursue their guerrilla strategy and sought to destroy as many economic and military targets as possible in the areas of operation where their troops infiltrated.[47] For the Sandinistas, the risk became greater and greater that the Contras would remove territories from government control. At the end of February, the General Offensive operation began. The FDN launched attacks in the north and centre of the country to penetrate the departments of Jinotega, Esteli, Matagalpa and Boaco, attacking Ocotal, Waslala and San Rafael del Norte, destroying economic and government infrastructure. On 24 March, the Diriangen Task Force seized San Rafael del Norte and kept it under its control for 24 hours.[48] ARDE attacked from Costa Rica, while MISURA and MISURATA forces were in action in the Atlantic region. All these Contra units received supplies by air to be able to maintain themselves inside Nicaragua.

The ARDE target was the city of San Juan del Norte, which from 6 April was under siege from approximately 350 fighters led by Tito Chamorro. The city, defended by 75 soldiers of the garrison, fell on 10 April after three days of fighting. ARDE's objective was then to continue to progress towards Bluefield to constitute a liberated area and form a provisional government under Calero's leadership.[49] Nevertheless, the

The commander of a BTR-60PB of the Mechanised Infantry Battalion of the EPS, negotiating the way forward for his vehicle, in the Jalapa region of early 1984. (Albert Grandolini Collection)

As the Contra-run campaigns intensified, in 1983 and 1984, the EPS was under ever greater pressure to train additional troops and bolster units deployed along the border to Honduras. This group of artillerists was photographed while undergoing training on Soviet-made 57mm ZiS-2 anti-tank guns. (Albert Grandolini Collection)

EPS took over the city on 17 April with aerial bombardment support and the ARDE troops withdraw to Costa Rica.[50]

In the north, the Contra offensive aimed to open supply routes to allow troops to remain inside the country for longer.[51] In this context, in April and May, the FDN carried out the largest infiltration operation of the conflict by bringing into Nicaragua nearly 6,000 combatants who reached the centre of the country and managed to remain there for several months. In June, about 3,000 Contras were also in the north of the country and attacked the cities of Ocotal, Waslala and San Rafael del Norte.[52] There were nearly 8,000 FDN fighters inside Nicaragua, some of them in the Matagalpa department. They were increasingly resupplied by air even if these supplies were often insufficient, as Edgar Chamorro acknowledged.[53] During these supply operations two C-47s were shot down by the Sandinistas in 1984, one near Quilali and the other near Matagalpa.[54]

The economic war against the Sandinista regime was not neglected.

A still from a video showing one of the – then – brand-new Mi-17s of the FAS, armed with four UB-32-57 pods for 57mm unguided rockets. The EPS became ever more reliant on helicopters for mobility as the fighting intensified and moved ever deeper into Nicaragua. (Pit Weinert Collection)

Table 5: FDN Structure, 1985

Position	Name
Commander and Chief-of-Staff	Enrique Bermudez
Regional Command Coordinator	Walter Calderon Lopez 'Toño'
General Staff	
G-1 (Personnel)	Harlie Duarte 'El Venado'
G-2 (Intelligence)	Donal Torres 'El Toro'
G-3 (Operations)	Luis Moreno Payan 'Mike Lima'
G-4 (Logistics)	Armando Lopez
G-5 (Psychological Warfare)	Rodolfo Ampié 'Invisible'
Central Commanders	
Air Operations	Juan Gomez
Counter-Intelligence	Ricardo Lau
MISURA Liaison	Justiciano Perez
Special Forces	Carlos José Guillen Salinas 'El Parajito'
Regional Commanders	
CR Nicarao	Jose Benito Bravo '*Commandante* Mack'
CR Segovia	Manuel Regama Acevedo '*Commandante* Auerliano'
CR Jorge Salazar	Juan Rivas Romero '*Commandante* Quiché'
CR Rafaela Herrera	Encarnacion Baldivia '*Commandante* Tigrillo'
CR Diriangen	'*Commandante* Dimas'
CR San Jacinto	Francisco Ruiz Castellon '*Commandante* Renato'
CR 15 September	Luis Fley Gonzalez '*Commandante* Johnson'
CR Juan Castro Castro	Jose Gaelano Rodas '*Commandante* Tiro al Blanco'
CR Alonso Irias	Abelardo Zelraya Chavarria '*Commandante* Ivan'
CR Andres Castro	Francisco Baldivia Chavarria '*Commandante* Dimas de Trigrillo'
CR Salvador Perez	Oscar Sobalvarro Garcia '*Commandante* Ruben'
CR Santiago Meza	Justo Pastor Meza Aguilar '*Commandante* Denis'
CR Pedro Joaquin Gonzalez	Rudy Zelaya Zeledon '*Commandante* Douglas'
CR Jose Dolores Estrada	Marcos Orlando Navarro Carrasco '*Commandante* Dimas Negro'

On 1 June, 600 FDN Contras seized Ocotal where they destroyed various economic facilities.[55] At the end of the year, an offensive was launched in the regions of San Rafael del Norte, San Juan del Río Coco, Waslala and Pantasma to prevent the harvest of coffee, a major export product for the economy. The defence of the harvest and the roads leading to the plantations required the mobilization of thousands of militiamen and volunteers in the departments of Jinotega and Matagalpa. In November, the government plantation of La Sorpresa, 60km north of Matagalpa, was attacked and severely damaged. Following this attack, the Contras organized ambushes on the roads leading to La Sopresa and succeeded in killing various Sandinista leaders on their way to the attacked farm. In the following days, they attacked another plantation in Los Angeles and then headed to Jinotega and Matagalpa.[56]

In 1984, the Contras benefited from the tactical initiative in all areas of operation. Their attacks were not only land-based, but they also launched maritime and air attacks against EPS patrol boats. In March 1984, in the Gulf of Fonseca, three EPS sailors were killed and three others wounded in one of these attacks.[57] This year marked the height of the Contra danger for the Sandinista regime and the leader of the FDN did not hesitate to announce that it would soon fall.[58]

Added to the increasing pressure of the Contra forces against the Sandinista government was the development of the CIA covert actions which were more and more daring. At the end of 1983, Navy Seals from USS *Gallery* laid mines in Nicaragua's most important harbours, Corinto, Puerto Sandino, and Bluefield, to impede oil imports that were vital to the country's economy. On 3 January 1984, a Japanese ship was hit by one of these mines in the port of Corinto. On 25 February, fishing vessels were damaged in the port of Bluefield. A dozen ships from six different countries were finally damaged by these naval mines.[59] The Sandinista government protested on 9 April 1984 and went to the International Court of Justice in The Hague accusing the US government of mining its ports and supporting Contra terrorism.[60]

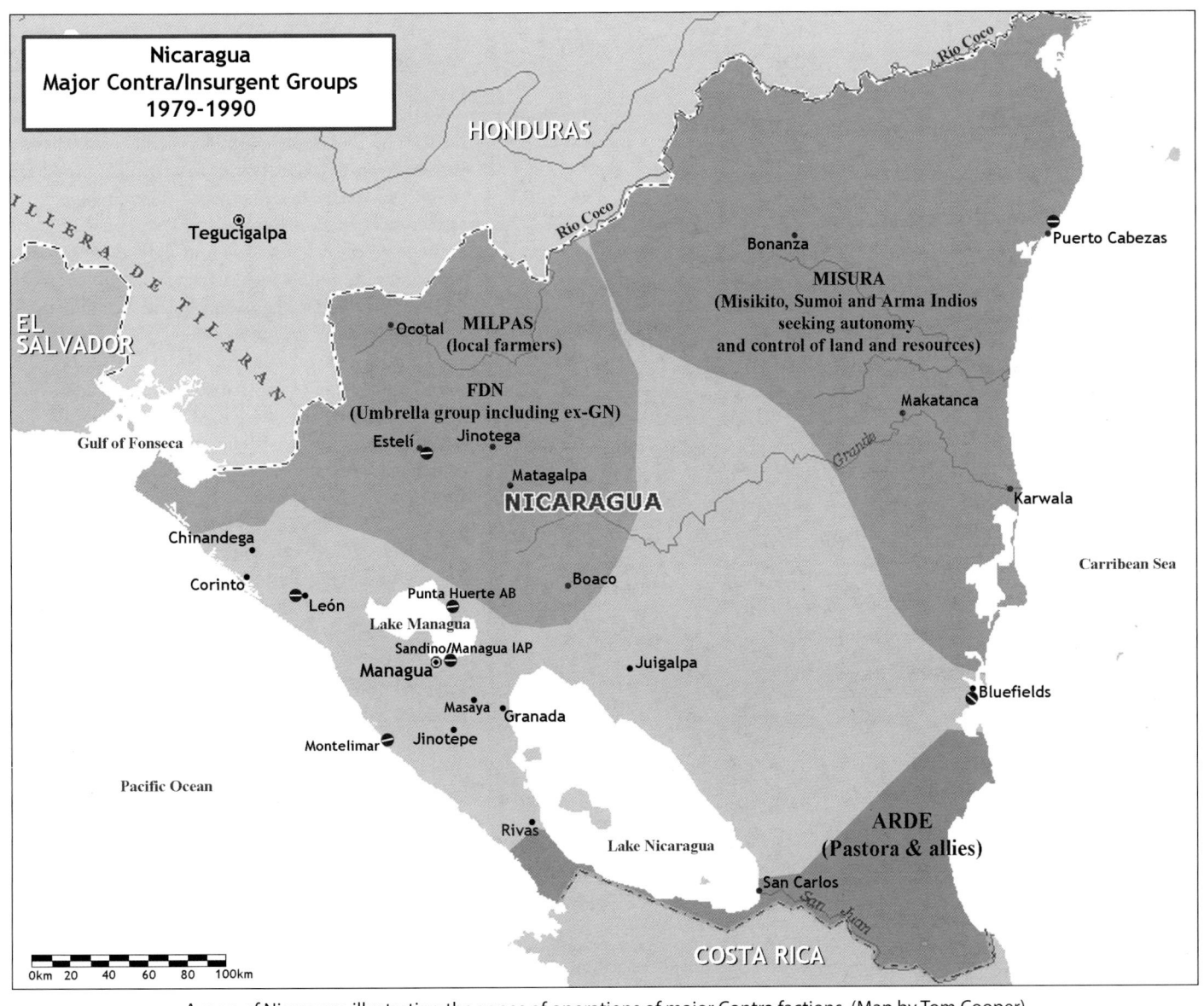

A map of Nicaragua illustrating the zones of operations of major Contra factions. (Map by Tom Cooper)

Contras Divided

The military rise of the Contras was coupled with a political offensive conducted under the aegis of the CIA. The Agency was aware that FDN leaders still had a poor image among the Nicaraguan population due to their brutality and Somozist past. First, they obtained the resignation of former GN officers such as Emilio Echeverry or Ricardo Lau.[61]

The US advisors still wanted a link between the FDN and Eden Pastora. ARDE's claimed independence prevented an effective fight because it refused to coordinate its actions with those of the FDN. Nevertheless, Pastora received support from the CIA, which provided a helicopter to ARDE to bomb San Juan del Norte.[62] In early 1984 however, the Costa Rican authorities informed ARDE that it was no longer welcome in the country. Pastora then planned to transport his men to Honduras and join forces with the FDN. In exchange, he asked for the departure of the command of the FDN from all the ex-GN and proposed to become the C-in-C of all the Contra forces. The Honduran military and the CIA were in favour of this solution, but FDN leaders refused it. The final decision rested with the US, who had full control over the FDN. For them, if Pastora was a very popular figure in Nicaragua, he nevertheless had the disadvantage of having left-wing ideas and especially of being unpredictable. They therefore finally found in favour of the FDN and stopped funding ARDE. On May 29, Pastora was the victim of a bomb attack. If not killed, he was seriously injured and withdrew from the ARDE in June.[63] The latter disintegrated and the Contras of the Southern Front approached the FDN while organizing themselves in the *Bloque Opositor del Sur* (Southern Opposition Bloc or BOS) first under the authority of Fernando Chamorro and then Alfredo César.[64]

The failure of the merger between the FDN and ARDE opened up a series of difficulties for the Contra cause. The attempted assassination of Pastora had an impact on the situation in the Atlantic region. The division had always been present among the indigenous Contras. If Fagoth was a supporter of armed struggle, other leaders did not see it that way. The criticism of his dictatorial behaviour was amplified by the appearance of ARDE, which seduced Miskitos like Rivera. The latter contacted Eden Pastora and joined him in Costa Rica, where he claimed for himself and his group the name MISURATA.[65] The dissension was violent as Rivera denounced MISURA's alliance with the GNs while Fagoth stigmatized the "infiltrated communists of MISURATA and ARDE." It also turned into a settling of scores and many protesters within the MISURA were executed.

The crisis in the leadership of the Miskito movement also reflected a political and military deadlock. While MISURA's forces inflicted casualties on the Sandinistas when they were on the border, the situation was quite different in the coastal area, and even more so in

Contra troops during a break in the fighting in central Nicaragua of 1984. Just as the war began developing in their favour, in 1984, the insurgents lost their Costa Rican support, and thus the ability to sandwich the Sandinistas by simultaneous attacks from two strategic directions. (Albert Grandolini Collection)

the Rosita and Bonanza mountains. The Contra Miskitos then had to fight several days march from the border, in areas now uninhabited due to population displacement, then crossing for days through the rainforest or savannah. In addition, in the mining area, they had to fight in a region where Sandinista troops were stationed who could count on the support of a Metis peasantry aligned to the government. In July 1982, the attack on the El Salto Grande dam in Bonanza by the Contras was defeated by the MPS, while the Contra attempt to seize Puerto Cabezas was also a failure.[66]

The experience of the Tronquera fighting in 1984 was even worse. Concerned about showing its military know-how and obtaining more resources from the US, MISURA headquarters recruited several hundred guerrillas to try to storm the entrenched camp that allowed the EPS to control the entire border region from San Carlos to Cabo Gracias to Dios and protected the road that leads from Puerto Cabezas to the mines and then to the Pacific region. The various troops involved in the operation approached their objective and found themselves at dawn, in the open, near the security perimeter of the Tronquera. Immediately spotted, they were caught under fire by automatic weapons served by soldiers protected by barbed wire networks and trenches. They suffered very heavy losses and most fled in complete disorder.[67]

The fighting in 1982 and 1983 was therefore particularly difficult for the Miskito fighters and the setbacks caused both fear of betrayal and discouragement. MISURA found itself unable to establish itself near the major cities of the Atlantic coast and to give an insurrectional aspect to the discontent of the local population.[68]

In the whole Atlantic region there were soon no more than a few thousand poorly armed fighters, whether Indians from MISURA and MISURATA or ARDE supporters, to face the Sandinista troops equipped with artillery and aviation. Despite the EPS firepower and the limited success of the Indigenous fighters' operations, the Sandinista authorities remained confronted with the hostility of the population.[69] The Atlantic region thus remained in a frozen situation.

Faced with the military dead end that was emerging, some argued that the armed struggle should be abandoned in order to defend the interests of the Atlantic region alone. While the defence of religion or opposition to the Sandinista agrarian policy of the Contra Miskitos was shared by other anti-Sandinista groups, the Miskitos did not place their struggle within a national framework, but an exclusively regional framework. Their objective was not to overthrow the government of Managua, an essential difference with the rest of the Contra formations. Moreover, the Miskitos were suspicious of these groups. If they accepted the material sent by the FDN, they were reluctant to link with them which they considered to be "Spanish" in the same way as the Sandinistas. Relations with the FDN were difficult because they did not take into account the particularities of the Atlantic region and were paternalistic towards the Miskitos, whose problems and claims seemed secondary to them.[70]

Pastora's withdrawal changed the situation, leaving Rivera and MISURATA isolated. Rivera then contacted the Sandinista government and in December 1984, he began talks with Comandante Luis Carrión in Colombia and then in Mexico. However, negotiations failed when Rivera called for the withdrawal of the Sandinistas from the Atlantic region.[71] These talks nevertheless showed the deep division that existed between the Contra forces, a division that was a factor of weakness in the face of Sandinista power. But more serious events for the Contras were taking place thousands of kilometres away in Washington.

In the United States, when it finally learned the CIA's role in laying mines in Nicaraguan ports, Congress was horrified. It considered this to be an act of war that endangered the lives of civilians. It therefore refused to grant the $21 million requested by the Reagan administration and adopted a new amendment (Boland II) that prohibited any further aid to the Contras.[72] It only authorized $27 million in humanitarian aid in the form of food and medical equipment. For the Speaker of the House of Representatives, the decision of Congress meant that the Contra War was "dead."[73] While Enrique Bermudez expected a quick victory on the condition that US aid would continue, the loss of this support was quickly felt.[74] MISURATA was negotiating with the Sandinista government while Daniel Ortega travelled to Moscow to ask for $200 million in assistance. Above all, the EPS took the military initiative on the ground.

6

THE SANDINISTA COUNTER-OFFENSIVE (1985-1986)

As soon as they came to power, the Sandinistas built a powerful conventional army because they believed that the main threat was direct intervention by the United States. But this force was inadequate to cope with the emergence and development of Contra activity. Against this new threat, which appeared to be increasingly serious, the EPS had to acquire a counter-insurgency doctrine and troops adapted for its application, otherwise there was a great risk of losing the war and therefore power.

The EPS Counter-Insurgency Strategy

The Sandinista leaders took time to take the Contra threat seriously. For them, the latter were only mercenaries and those nostalgic for Somoza who served as the vanguard for a US invasion. In 1983, Tomas Borge, the Minister of the Interior, stated that the incursions of the Contras might be a prelude to "a military intervention by the United States, which would constitute a grave threat to the independence and sovereignty of the Central American countries and to world peace and security."[1]

Attacks on northern cities, particularly Jalapa, to form a Contra territorial base were easily repelled by the EPS in conventional fighting.[2] Managua therefore remained focused on the danger of a US invasion and neglected the fight against Contra incursions, which were perceived as diversionary manoeuvres to attract troops out of the Pacific area. The fight against the Contras was initially entrusted only to the *Lucha contra bandas somozistas* (Anti Somozista military patrols) units, made up of small groups of soldiers led by experienced guerrillas who settled in Wiwilí, Río Blanco and Waslala.

To cover the vast northern regions, the EPS had only poorly armed MPS and reserve battalions that had received only limited training.[3] In RM 6, there were 12,000 militiamen, most of whom were agricultural workers or cooperative peasants, while reserve battalions were composed of volunteers, often young people from poor urban areas. In the Atlantic coast, in October 1982, the 80-15 reservist battalion was composed of craftsmen and shoemakers while in early 1983, in Rio Blanco, in the department of Jinotega, there was a reserve battalion of the Sandinista Youth.[4] These forces were insufficient to contain the Contras and Lieutenant Fidel Tinoco Zeledon, who commanded a Sandinista patrol to hunt them down in the mountains of the regions of Wiwili, Aguas Calientes, Kilambé, Plan de Grama and San José de Bocay between 30 December 1980 to 29 June 1982, admitted in his diary what little success he had encountered.[5]

Under these conditions, the Contras had little difficulty dominating in the regions where they operated. They could therefore attack with impunity the structures set up by the authorities since the revolution but also by murdering volunteers who carried out medical and educational tasks for the population. In Quilali, in 1983, 12 of 33 primary schools were abandoned by Sandinistas who could not protect them and four were burned by the Contras.[6] Gradually, the Sandinistas and their supporters living in the countryside fled to the cities, as did some rural people who feared the growing insecurity. For fear of the Contras, a part of the population, initially in favour of the FSLN, turned away from the revolution. In 1984, the EPS leaders were finally aware of the danger posed by the Contras, as *Commandante* Manuel Salvatierra who oversaw Sandinista forces in the northern region acknowledged : "We realize that this war is going to continue for a long time."[7]

The EPS' increasing emphasis on 'forward defence' along the border to Honduras, resulted in the continuous growth of the importance of MPS battalions. While enthusiastic to engage the Contras, the irregulars were poorly-armed and too few, and thus unable to prevent further insurgent infiltrations on their own. (Albert Grandolini Collection)

Humberto Ortega and Joaquin Cuadra Lacayo, at a meeting with the National Directorate, announced that the war against the Contras could be lost without a change in strategy.[8] Border guard forces were unable to block all of the border with Honduras, which was nearly 700km long, forcing the EPS to defend mainly urban centres such as Matagalpa, Jinotega, Estelí, Jalapa or Waslala. Humberto Ortega then developed the concept of strategic defeat of the insurgents, which consisted of withdrawing the initiative from the Contras and preventing them from developing as a military and political force.[9]

The Sandinista leaders, all of whom were ex-guerrillas, knew from experience that mobility was the guerrillas' primary asset, as it compensated for low firepower. The formation of Contra-controlled areas might be a solution for the government forces, which would then have the advantage in direct fighting against insurgents who would defend these areas. But the EPS did not want to repeat the mistakes of the GN, which in this situation alienated the population through indiscriminate tactical operations where collateral damage against civilians had been significant. The main tactic of the EPS was therefore to defend the country as far forward as possible, i.e. not to let the Contras rest both inside the country and at their base in Honduras. This "advanced defence" strategy aimed to keep the Contras out of Nicaragua by aggressively engaging them along the border and thus preventing them from infiltrating the country.[10]

To implement this strategy, in May 1984 the Sandinista leadership set up the Supreme Council for the Defence of the Fatherland and Regional Defence and Security Councils in the RMs. The mission of these organization was to better coordinate the structures of the EPS, MINT and the State in order to implement defence plans such as the "From Pomares to Fonseca" plan, which aimed to combine all the State's initiatives around defence needs. In RMs 1 and 6, the

Even the large-scale infiltration by the Contras of central and eastern Nicaragua in 1984 failed to force the EPS to react by deploying its most powerful combat units: the five armoured battalions remained in strategic reserve, expecting a possible US invasion. Their crews thus continued their routine training on T-55s, and frequently even ran large-scale exercises to train for defence against a US attack. (Albert Grandolini Collection)

A rare view of a BTS-2 armoured recovery vehicle, at least two of which were assigned to each of the EPS' armoured battalions. (Albert Grandolini Collection)

place.[12] In the Jalapa Valley, just beside the border with Honduras, farmers received weapons while trenches and pits were built around the houses.[13] The aim was to form a protection belt along the border. In Jalapa, which had a population of nearly 15,000, one third of the population also participated in civil defence, including patrols around the city.[14] Population displacements were also used to combat the Contras. These operations made it possible to deprive them of their support among the civilian population but also to create areas where the EPS could operate freely and used its firepower without fear of civilian damage. In early 1985, many population displacement operations took place in the north of the country.[15]

For its part, the DGSE was setting up a network of informants to identify the development of the Contra infrastructure. This allowed them, for example, in early 1983 to dismantle an ARDE group in Managua and in June 1984 to arrest Contra supporters in Matagalpa and Chinandega where the DGSE discovered crates of C-4 plastic explosives and several light antitank weapons in a home.[16] Operation *Llovizna*, in November 1985, led to the arrest of 150 Contras in the departments of Matagalpa and Jinotega. The DGSE also infiltrated agents into the Contras in Honduras. In December 1983, thanks to informants in Tegucigalpa, the EPS inflicted severe losses on the Diriangen Task Force in La Vigía and El Cuá. About a hundred Contra fighters were killed and 200 wounded.[17] To fight this infiltration, the FDN had to set up a military police and a counter-intelligence service under the command of Lieutenant Rodolfo Ampié. He thus discovered seven Sandinista officers and soldiers infiltrated in the FDN in order to assassinate Bermúdez.[18] The DGSE also promoted the desertion of Contra fighters, in particular by relying on the amnesty proclaimed in 1985 by the government. This led to the defection of José Efrén Mondragón, head of the José Dolores Estrada CR, who joined the Sandinistas in June 1985.[19] The DGSE successfully fulfilled its mission of protecting the regime by preventing the Contras from establishing themselves in large cities and on the Pacific coast and also avoided any attack against Managua and the capitals of the departments.

While the entire State and Sandinista organizations mobilized to fight the Contras, the main role in this fight was played by the EPS, which equipped itself with the tactics and combat training necessary to take the initiative again.

most affected by Contra activity, the National Directorate assigned responsibility for the fight against the Contras to Commander Luis Carrion.

The Sandinistas first increased border protection with 44 companies of border guard troops, about 5,000 men who were reinforced with equipment in war zones. To prevent the Contras from entering and establishing themselves in the country, it was necessary to cut them off from the local population. To do this, the authorities relied on population supervision organizations such as the CDS.[11] Although mainly located in urban areas, the CDS were also present in rural villages and cooperative farms and provided information on Contra movements. The inhabitants were also organized in local self-defence structures that were set up in 1983 with the formation of *Cooperativas de Autodefensa* (Autodefence Cooperatives) and 80 *Compañias Permanentes Territoriales* (Permanent Territorial Companies) formed by peasants and militiamen from the areas where the fighting took

Sandinista Counter-Insurgency Forces

According to the head of the FDN intelligence services, Rodolfo Ampié, it was the head of the Cuban military mission in Managua, General Ochoa, who suggested the formation of specialized counter-insurgency units based on his experience in Ethiopia. Sandinista guerrilla veterans knew the effectiveness of large military units of battalion size, such as the GN Combat Battalion, with good tactical mobility to allow them to surround the enemy and push them into battle before destroying them with their firepower or air support. The EPS, based on the SMP, which allowed a better distribution of forces, created *Batallones de Lucha Irregular* (Irregular Warfare Battalions or BLI) on a national level and *Batallones de Lucha Cazador* (Light Hunter Battalions or BLC) at the local level.

The 21 BLCs, controlled by the brigade commander of the local EPS, were made up of farmers who, instead of carrying out their SMP in other parts of the territory, were mobilized on the spot. Each EPS brigade thus had a BLC or even two in some regions. Knowing both the geography and the local population, they were responsible for conducting counter-insurgency operations in a limited geographical area. Designed to hunt down small Contra forces, their constant activity was to prevent the enemy from establishing bases in their areas.

The *Batallon de Lucha Irregular* (BLI) were responsible for counter-insurgency at the national level and could be deployed in all RMs where the Contras operated. Initially, all BLIs were directly controlled by the national EPS HQ, which could deploy them anywhere in the country. The authorities found this system too centralized and subsequently decided to allocate the BLIs to the two RMs most threatened by the Contras, RM 5 and 6. Nevertheless, the Ministry of Defence retained the right to temporarily reassign BLIs between Military Regions as required.[20]

The BLIs, operating throughout the RM, had the task of operating against high concentrations of Contras. For soldiers, this often meant extended periods away from their garrisons and therefore required a significant support infrastructure, particularly for travel. The first BLI formed was the BLI Simon Bolivar.[21] This was involved in the first action of this type of unit, on 11 May 1983, with a reserve Battalion of the Sandinista Youth and another composed of inhabitants of the eastern and western districts of Managua against a Contra camp led by "Renato" at the confluence of the rivers Coco and Bocay. Some of the troops were flown by helicopter to Rio Amaka, 25km from the camp, from where they walked through the jungle to get closer. The camp was attacked by mortars, particularly the airstrip where a C-47 aircraft managed to take off and launched two rockets against the EPS men. Nevertheless, the BLI managed to seize the airstrip while the Contras crossed the Rio Coco to take refuge in Honduras from where they fired machine guns and mortars on the Sandinistas.[22] This first success promised others.

In 1986 there were 12 BLIs with about 700 men each.[23] A 13th BLI was formed in 1987. These units could rely on 44 Operational Support Bases with reservists and militiamen from the Pacific region,

A gathering of the Contras in one of their bases inside Honduras in 1986: due to the activity of the small but very active EPS COIN teams, they often found their way into Nicaragua blocked by mines and other obstacles. (Photo by J B P)

Through 1986, the ARDE and the FDN found even their bases inside Honduras under pressure from the EPS: this photograph shows a Soviet-made 12.7mm DShK ('Dushka') heavy machine gun being used to defend a forward base. (Photo by J B P)

while 115 MPS companies were mobilized in war zones to support the BLIs and blockaded threatened areas. Approximately 35,000 to 40,000 combatants were involved in the fight against the Contras.[24]

Table 6: BLIs
Designation
BLI 'Simón Bolívar'
BLI 'Germán Pomares'
BLI 'General Francisco Estrada'
BLI 'Coronel Santos López'
BLI 'General Miguel Ángel Ortez'
BLI 'Coronel Rufo Marrín'
BLI 'General Juan Pablo Umanzor'
BLI 'Farabundo Marti'
BLI 'Coronel Sócrates Sandino'
BLI 'Coronel Ramón Raudales'
BLI 'General Juan Gregorio Colindres'
BLI 'General Pedro Altamirano'
BLI 'Heriberto Reyes'

In addition to the BLIs and BLCs, the Sandinistas employed a variety of small units as special forces in reconnaissance and strike missions. In 1982, the EPS set up an in-depth reconnaissance unit, the *Tropas Pedro Altamirano* (TPA) led by Miguel Angel Amador, which played an essential role during Operation *Soberania* against the ARDE in May 1985.[25] However, the most common special units were the *Pequeñas Unidades Fuerzas de Especiales* (Small Special Forces Units or PUFES). They were created on 25 October 1985 and some of the combatants were trained in Cuba.[26] There were three PUFES companies of 120 men each, but the basic structure of these units was a team of five people, capable of uniting with other units for larger operations. Their role was to spot Contra units and could harass them by laying M18 Claymore mines in their path, forcing them to stop marching during the day and move only at night.[27]

While developing counter-insurgency units, the EPS was also developing combat tactics to deal with the Contras. The PUFES were responsible for locating large enemy concentrations and, with the help of border guards, monitoring infiltration routes. To locate the Contras, the EPS also used technology by forming the *Técnica Operativa*, which consisted of trucks equipped with direction finding devices to locate the radios used by the Contra units.

On the basis of intelligence obtained by intercepting radio messages or DGSE information, the PUFES would search for Contra units when they crossed the border. They thus provided accurate information on the size, activity, location and equipment of the opponent. Once this information was obtained, larger units, BLC or BLI were sent to intercept and destroy the infiltrators. These units formed a military cordon around a general area where the Contras were detected and then, complemented by artillery and air support, could encircle the enemy and annihilate them.[28]

The essential element in the advanced defence strategy implemented by the EPS was speed and mobility in order to be able to hit opposing forces as quickly as possible after they were detected. On this point, the Contras took advantage of the particular geography of the highlands of central Nicaragua, where thick forests and steep hills dominated. Most importantly, Nicaragua then had only 1,665km of paved roads, or about 30% of what was the north-south segment of the Pan-American Highway. The remaining unpaved roads, which constituted the majority of the country's roads, were difficult to use during the rainy season from May to October. This situation was a handicap for the EPS mobility. Thus the main artillery support, the BM-21 multiple rocket launcher mounted on a truck and capable of rapidly saturating an area, was hampered by this defective road network, which prevented it from deploying in the highlands and thus limited the areas where the EPS forces could receive its support.[29]

To overcome its problems, the EPS made the helicopter the main weapon in its counter-insurgency response. It provided firepower, high tactical mobility and logistical support. The acquisition of Mi-25 helicopters was decisive in this respect.[30] This sophisticated helicopter could fly at nearly 320km per hour, carry bombs and could be equipped with significant numbers of rockets. It also allowed troops to move quickly and hindered the mobility of the opponent who, when detected on the ground, became prey to the powerful fire of the Mi-25. It was used in 1984 to bomb the Contras near the border with Costa Rica and then in the vicinity of Esteli, which was threatened by the FDN, and in the Chontales region. In December 1984, during Operation *Victorious December* the Sandinistas demonstrated the ability of Mi-8 helicopters to move, and Mi-25s to support, their troops. They started rolling up the Contras from the area some 70km north of Managua towards the border with Honduras and out of Jinotega Province. The

The establishment of the BLIs provided the EPS with a well-organized and well-led quick reaction force. Supported by intelligence obtained by the DGSE, and FAS helicopters, the irregulars – including female units – proved capable of running pursuits of infiltrating Contras lasting for several days, thus keeping their enemy under constant pressure. (Albert Grandolini Collection)

Mi-25, whose effectiveness was both military and psychological, became the terror of the Contras, who did not hesitate to offer a reward of one million dollars to the pilot of any Mi-25 who defected.[31]

Beginning in 1983, counter-insurgency tactics deployed by the EPS were implemented in the northern part of the country. Patrols were constantly on the ground, sometimes for weeks at a time, searching for Contra units to attack them as soon as possible. The Sandinistas took advantage of their numerical superiority for this purpose, since in the spring of 1983, several thousand soldiers from the BLC and BLI were in the region, particularly in the department of Jinotega under the direction of Alvaro Baltodano.[32] This increase in EPS activity was reflected in a rise in clashes with the Contras.

During 1984, the FAS began deploying its Mi-8/17 and Mi-25 helicopters in a growing number of 'Fire-Force' style of operations (famous from the Rhodesian War of the 1970s). This group of seven 'Hips' was photographed while underway to deploy ground troops around an enemy unit detected and pinned down by Mi-25s in northern central Nicaragua: notable is the heavy rocket armament of every helicopter, consisting of six UB-32-57 rocket pods. (Albert Grandolini Collection)

The Contras on the Defensive

The implementation of the advanced defence strategy was developing at a time when the US Congress ended official assistance to the Contras. This situation obviously had an impact on their fighting capacity and since the end of 1984, attacks on coffee plantations in the provinces of Matagalpa and Jinotega had been reduced in number.[33] The Contras, aware that they could no longer overthrow Sandinista power with a military victory, therefore sought to avoid direct clashes with the EPS in favour of attacks on economic infrastructure and thus undermined the population's confidence in the government. In the first half of 1985, they destroyed 14 high-voltage lines, 12 cooperatives, three tobacco depots and two power plants.[34]

Nevertheless, as in the previous year, the Contras continued their infiltration operations inside Nicaragua. In January 1985, they entered the department of Jinotega but instead of attacking isolated farms, they advanced on the main road, destroying bridges, many trucks and four electrical towers, depriving Jinotaga of electricity for three days.[35]

In July, Operation *Rebelion 85* began. The objective was to infiltrate thousands of fighters inside the country and to recover the territories lost since November 1984. One CR had to break the defensive lines established by the EPS and opened a corridor where the other CRs had to pass and relieve Sandinista pressure in the north. It was up to CR Jorge Salazar to infiltrate through the Matagalpa mountains to reach the regions of Boaco, Chontales and the centre of Zelaya, a mountainous and inaccessible area that became a refuge that had to be supplied by air.

The operation began with the attack on Trinidad and Sebaco led by the CRs Pedro Joaquin Gonzalez, Santiago Meza, Salvador Pérez and Larry McDonald. The offensive led to a combined and simultaneous action on San Isidro (Matagalpa department) by CR Santiago Meza, on La Trinidad (Esteli department) by CR Pedro Joaquin Gonzalez, ambushes in the Esteli area and the destruction of La Sirena bridge by CR José Dolores Estrada and the destruction of Sébaco bridge by CR Quilalí. A rear guard was placed on the heights of San Rafael del Norte to prevent the movement of the EPS during the retreat from Esteli. On 1 August, the FDN captured La Trinidad and cut off the Pan-American Highway for a day, but the EPS Mi-25 helicopters responded quickly while airlifted troops harassed the Contras who had to retreat. During these operations between La Sirena and Sébaco, the FDN's losses were severe: 202 dead, 409 wounded, 62 captured. On the same day as the attack on Trinidad, 500 Contra fighters attacked the Cuapa garrison in the department of Chontales.[36]

While Operation *Rebelion 85* allowed the infiltration of CR Jorge Salazar, this success could not hide the fact that the EPS resumed the tactical initiative and launched numerous attacks between November 1984 to mid-1985. In December 1984 and January 1985, these actions were concentrated in the Nueva Segovia region with the *Campaña Invierno* operation. The fighting continued in the following months and was most violent in April. The objective was to drive the Contras out from the north of the country and isolate those who had managed to infiltrate the country in remote areas. In May, the EPS captured the largest FDN base in the Jinotega region, forcing the Contras to take refuge in the isolated areas of the Boaco and Chontales departments.

The Jorge Salazar Task Force maintained a Contra presence in the eastern part of the Boaco department, the northwest part of the Chontales department and the west-central part of the Zelaya department, about 250km from the Honduran border. It had support among the population, which also allowed it to operate in the Matagalpa region. But these troops took care to attack only poorly defended and sparsely populated areas on the axis between Juigalpa and Rama. The objective of their attacks was only to destroy agricultural installations and created a climate of insecurity through assassinations, as in Boaco where 20 people were killed in May 1985.[37] They carefully avoided cities like Santo Domingo, which were strongly defended by superior Sandinista troops and which continued to patrol the region with the support of helicopters and artillery. Only Cuapa was taken by the Contras at the beginning of August.[38]

It is true that the EPS's response to the actions of the Contras in the centre of the country was strong. It sought, if not to destroy them,

An irregular of the BLI waiting to be picked up by a Mi-17 about to land in the background. (EPS via Tom Cooper)

The pilot of a Cessna 337 donning his parachute before the next sortie. The few remaining 'push-pull' aircraft frequently played a crucial role in locating concentrations of the Contras. (Albert Grandolini Collection)

to confined them in the depopulated jungle of Zelaya department.[39] To cut off the Contra forces from their support and thus suffocate them, thousands of peasants were displaced to be installed near the EPS garrisons. The elimination of the Contras was entrusted to a *Táctico Operacional Group*, composed of six battalions of BLIs and a group with 17 Mi-17 and Mi-25 who were specially trained to conduct Operation *Repunte 86*. The latter consisted of a series of attacks against the Contra troops in the centre of the country, which were gradually progressing in a complete arc to the Honduran border in the department of Jinotega. The EPS thus pushed the Contra forces, which, having lost the tactical initiative, only maintained small units inside the country.[40]

In all these EPS operations, combat helicopters played an important role with a devastating effect on the Contras. Thus in September 1985, when the FDN captured Santo Domingo, the Mi-25 counterattack was terrifying, killing 25 Contras with a single blow. They mainly prevented them from using large units, while forcing them to launch only night attacks for which they were not prepared, and caused significant losses, as the CR Jorge Salazar unit's attack against San Pedro de Lóvago in August 1985 when the four company leaders and 17 group leaders were killed.[41]

During *Repunte 86*, Honduran forces had to intervene to support the Contras. In August and September 1985 the FAH Super Mystére B.2s, F-86s and A-37s actively supported some 500 Contras involved in battle around Jalapa. After an attack by FAS Mi-8s and Mi-25s, the FAH supported the Contras with A-37 and F-86 sorties. During the fighting in the area, on 13 September, a FAH F-86 intercepted and damaged a Nicaraguan Mi-25, forcing it to make an emergency landing.

After hitting the FDN in the north and centre of the country, the EPS turned south. In this region, ARDE's attempt to seize Bluefield Bay in May 1985 turned into a disaster. Commanders "Tapo" and "Mano Negra" were killed during the fighting, which lasted four hours, and the Contras had to withdraw in disorder to Costa Rica.[42] The EPS then continued its offensive against ARDE with the Soberania Plan, which began on 26 May in the department of Rio San Juan. This operation led to the takeover of the headquarters of Pastora, the base of La Penca on 11 June. The EPS inflicted severe blows upon ARDE forces. At the beginning of June, their situation was so desperate that Pastora had to launch a call for help to the international community.[43] Nevertheless, Operation *Soberania* continued in July along the Rio San Juan and in August most of ARDE's forces took refuge in Costa Rica.

In the Atlantic region, MISURA forces were no longer able to carry out spectacular actions after the attack on the Tronquera in 1984. In this region, the fighting was reduced to a low-intensity attritional war until the end of the conflict, where the MISURA avoided facing the EPS directly to attack defenceless economic targets. On the military level, it no longer represented a danger to Sandinista power.[44]

At the end of 1985, the situation was precarious for the Contras. While the FDN was able to maintain troops in central Nicaragua, its few achievements had not been enough to reverse the successes of the EPS, which remained larger in number, better armed and made intensive use of Mi-25 helicopters. The Contras were then unable to carry out major coordinated operations likely to shake up power, let alone confront the Sandinistas. The volume of their losses illustrated the success of the Sandinista reaction. Indeed, while in 1982-1983, approximately 1,500 Contra fighters were killed, there were nearly 5,800 in 1984-1985, figures to which have to be added the thousands of wounded and mutilated.[45]

Sandinista Raids into Honduras

The Sandinistas knew they could never win the war as long as the Contras could escape and rest and be resupplied freely just across the border in Honduras. Managua also knew that it could not obtain the closure of the Contra bases from its neighbour, which were supported by the Honduran military and especially by the United States. According to Ampié, it was General Ochoa who suggested to the EPS leaders that they organized incursions into Honduras to destroy these bases. According to some observers, the objective was to destroy the Contra military forces before the end of 1985.[46]

It was by pursuing Contra forces taking refuge in Honduras that Sandinista incursion operations began in February 1985 when the EPS mobilized the 61st Brigade in the El Rosario area. In response, the FDN gathered all its available units and launched Operation *Cangrejo* on 4 March. After four days of fighting, the Contras seized the command post of the 61st Brigade and captured some 120mm mortars.⁴⁷ The Sandinista government took advantage of this attack to denounce an invasion of Nicaragua by Honduran troops.

On 1 May 1985, between the hamlets of Cuanito and Playa Hermosa, 122mm guns and BM-21 batteries delivered large volumes of fire against the Las Vegas salient where the main FDN bases in Honduras were located. Then, the EPS launched a major offensive with border guard units, the BLIs Santos Lopez and Rufo Marin, with a thousand soldiers gathered near Teocacinte. The fighting against the CR José Dolores Estrada in Cerro El Súbico was particularly violent.⁴⁸ The Sandinista attack was a surprise for the Contras who suffered significant losses.⁴⁹

In June 1985, it was to the south that the EPS extended beyond its borders by making a few incursions into Costa Rica to destroy ARDE bases. Sandinista forces also did not hesitate to bomb these bases from across the border and Costa Rican President Luis Alberto Monge protested in front of the OAS against these incursions.⁵⁰

The Las Vegas area, the starting point for many FDN incursions, and home to nearly 15,000 Contra fighters in the fall of 1985, emerged as a prime target for the EPS. To prepare their attack against this area, the Sandinistas built a road in the Las Piedras area and another in the El Rosario area to transport multiple BM-21 rocket launchers. In September 1985, these BM-21s, with a range of 20km, bombarded the Las Vegas area while five Mi-17 and Mi-25 helicopters were in action. The air attack was repelled by four F-86 Sabres and Super Mystères of the FAH. On the ground, the Contras also managed to repel the EPS troops. Nevertheless, the FDN bases were moved to the Yamales area, 30km from the border, and out of reach of the Sandinista artillery.⁵¹

In March 1986, the Sandinistas launched a major offensive against the FDN's Military Instruction Center in Honduran territory. They seized the outpost of Boca de Yamales but had to face the forces of CR Jorge Salazar 1 in the El Papaleo sector and eventually retreat. On this occasion, the Contras captured 10 soldiers from BLIs Santos Lopez

A Cessna 337 of the FAS, armed with Matra F1 pods for unguided rockets, on the way into the next reconnaissance sortie, early during the war. Notable are a C-47 and an AT-33A (left and right in the background, respectively). (Albert Grandolini Collection)

The crew of FAS Mi-8/17s and Mi-25s posing for a group photograph before the next mission: in a series of high-speed operations run in cooperation with diverse BLIs, they caused severe losses to the Contras through 1984 and 1985. (Albert Grandolini Collection)

and German Pomares who were used by the Honduran authorities to denounce the Sandinista incursion.⁵²

On 26 March 1986, about a thousand Sandinistas gathered near Teotecacinte were involved in incursions into Honduras, sometimes as far as 10km across the border.⁵³ The fighting then concentrated around Arenales, forcing the Honduran army to send an infantry battalion to the area.⁵⁴ Exchanges of fire took place between EPS troops and Honduran soldiers, and a FAH helicopter was even hit by shots from a Sandinista machine gun.⁵⁵ Washington then assisted its Honduran ally and USAF pilots used four Chinook and ten Huey helicopters to transport a Honduran artillery and infantry battalion into the Las Vegas salient.⁵⁶ Washington also supplied Tegucigalpa with helicopters and means of transport as well as artillery pieces deployed to the Capire region.⁵⁷

General Arnaldo T. Ochoa Sanchez, veteran of the Bay of Pigs battle, the leader of Cuban contingents in Angola of 1975-1976 and during the Ogaden War (Ethiopia-Somalia) in 1977-1978 and bearer of the Hero of the Revolution medal, served as the top military adviser in Managua of 1983-1984. He was the initiator of the FAS operations against the Contra bases in Honduras. (Albert Grandolini Collection)

A battery of BM-21 multiple rocket launchers of the FAS opening the assault on the Las Vegas salient in May 1985. (Albert Grandolini Collection)

A platoon of Sandinista special troops crossing the Coco River during another foray over the border into Honduras in 1985-1986. (Albert Grandolini Collection)

At the end of 1986, the EPS reached a new level in its strategy of incursion into Honduras. Indeed, Operation *Unidad Indestrucible*, which then began, brought together six BM-21s, two batteries of 122mm and 152mm howitzers, nine BLI battalions, special troops, and border guard battalions, under the command of Colonel Salvatierra. The attack, which still targeted the Las Vegas salient, began with artillery fire across the front line from the mouth of the Rio Capire to Banco Grande on the Rio Coco. Then the infantry went on the attack and pressed the first line of defence of the Contras, which withdrew to the hills of Zepeda and La Loca. The EPS advanced from El Tablazo and El Súbico while CR Jorge Salazar 5 reinforced the Contra defence, which dug trenches and fortified hills with Browning M2 machine guns, mortars and Supra anti-personnel mines.

On December 2, the EPS launched a new attack against 1,200 Contra fighters. After intense artillery bombardment, the Sandinistas led a frontal assault against the enemy defences. A unit of the EPS seized part of Zepeda hill but a counter-attack pushed them back. On the night of December 3, the Contras launched a counter-attack against BLI Ramon Raudales with 900 men. The EPS did not have enough troops to resist and retreated. On 4 December, the EPS regained the positions lost on the 3rd, and on the 5th returned to the offensive launching 17 attacks against the positions of CR Jorge Salazar 5. By trying to attack from the right flank, the Sandinista troops then made contact with units of the Honduran army. On the same day some A-37 Dragonflies of the FAH bombarded the EPS forces as well as the command post in Congoja and the road to Wiwili. The Sandinistas then withdrew to Nicaragua.[58] For the first time, Nicaraguan troops inside Honduras came into sustained contact with Honduran troops and inflicted casualties.

In 1986, faced with the growing power of the EPS, the Contras were forced to defend themselves. The high mobility of the BLIs forced them to move constantly, to disperse into small groups and were unable to settle in without being detected and attacked. The war of attrition then turned against them. They nevertheless continued to carry out actions, but of lower intensity than in previous years, only trying to maintain a physical presence through harassment operations in the departments of Nueva Segovia, Madriz, Esteli, Jinotega, and Matagalpa.[59]

The decline in Contra military activity was reflected in their inability to disrupt the coffee harvest that year and the withdrawal of almost all of their forces in Honduras, with the exception of 3,000 Jorge Salazar Task Force fighters who moved to the departments of Zelaya, Chontales and Boaco. For its part, the EPS seemed more powerful than ever, particularly because of its control of the sky, thanks to the Mi-25, and the effectiveness of its

Honduran troops in a position near the border with Nicaragua in 1985: by the following year, they became involved in regular clashes with diverse FAS units attacking Contra bases inside Honduras. (US Army)

forces and its counter-insurgency strategy. However, the Sandinistas not only used the military solution to weaken the Contras, they also knew how to play the political weapon, especially in the Atlantic region where the military activity of the MISURA became reduced from 1985 onwards.

The Pacification of the Atlantic Region

In the Atlantic region, after the failure of negotiations with Rivera in 1984, the Sandinistas continued discussions with local actors. They were aware of the regional nature of the Miskitos' struggle, who did not want to seize power in Nicaragua but just to obtain political and cultural autonomy. They therefore decided to adopt a more flexible policy. In 1985, Borge, the Minister of the Interior, became the main Sandinista responsible for the Atlantic region. In June 1985, he announced that persons displaced in 1982 could return to their villages along the Rio Coco. He also benefited from the lack of structures of the Indian rebels; the Miskitos forces were led by local leaders who each command about 100 men and these leaders, if they were loyal either to MISURA or MISURATA, acted autonomously. Borge offered them an amnesty and the right to ensure local security with their men and weapons and many warlords accepted this proposal.[60] Commander Eduardo Pantin of the MISURA met Sandinista Deputy Commander Jose Gonzalez in Puerto Cabezas on 17 May to sign a ceasefire. In the following months, other Miskitos commanders signed identical agreements.[61] The FSLN also offered guarantees to exiles in Honduran territory who were gradually returning. Borge's skilful policy made it possible to restore relative calm in the Atlantic region and established a precarious peace.

The change in the political orientation of the FSLN in the Atlantic region led to the promulgation in September 1987 of the Autonomous Statute of the Atlantic Coast Regions of Nicaragua. The government transformed the vast Caribbean territory into two distinct regions with their own fiscal resources and local autonomy: the North Atlantic Autonomous Region (RAAN) and the South Atlantic Autonomous Region (RAAS).

Faced with this change in Sandinista policy, the Assembly of the Indigenous People of the Atlantic Coast, the structure that led all anti-Sandinista Miskitos, decided to unify its 4,000 fighters into a new organization, the KISAN.[62] Fagoth and Rivera refused to accept this decision and kept the names MISURA and MISURATA for their organizations. KISAN was more autonomous from the FDN and had Wycliffe Diego, a former Moravian pastor, as its leader. However, it failed to gather all the Contra Miskitos because shortly after its formation, six of its commanders entered into talks with the Sandinistas.[63] For his part, in 1986, Rivera clandestinely entered the Atlantic region where he was pursued by Sandinista troops, while Washington no longer provided any support to MISURATA.[64]

Outside the Atlantic region, the Sandinista government was seeking democratic legitimacy. The revolutionary government published the Political Parties Act in 1982 and created the Supreme Electoral Council, an independent body responsible for organizing elections in 1984. At that time, it hoped to see the formation of a loyal opposition that would accept Sandinista hegemony. For the 1984 elections, FSLN nominated Daniel Ortega and Sergio Ramirez as presidential candidates and called for the participation of the right-wing coalition formed within the Council of State in 1982, the Democratic Coalition of Nicaragua led by Arturo Cruz. But a few days before the elections, and apparently following a decision imposed by the United States, Cruz abandoned his candidacy stating that his participation would legitimize the elections and thus the probable victory of the Sandinistas. Daniel Ortega, was finally elected with 63% of the vote while the FSLN won the legislative elections with 67% of the votes and 61 seats out of 96 and 75% of the votes. The other political parties had more or less reluctantly played the role of the official opposition. A new Constitution drafted by the Assembly came into force in January 1987 with a highly centralized power in the hands of Daniel Ortega.[65]

7
BETWEEN WAR AND PEACE (1986-1988)

Emboldened by the results of the 1984 elections, and feeling safe in their position, in late 1985 the Sandinistas took the initiative again – both militarily and politically. The Contras were on the defensive. With Pastora's withdrawal, the Southern Front had almost ceased to exist, the Miskitos' forces were divided and no longer posed a military threat, while the FDN forces had mostly withdrawn to Honduras. But still supported by Washington, the Contras did not collapse and the war continued.

US Clandestine Support

The difficulties faced by the Contras from 1985 onwards were not only the result of the success of the Sandinista counter-insurgency strategy or political skill, but also of the decision in 1984 by Congress to cease US aid.

The Contras lacked military equipment, even such essentials as boots and ponchos for guerrilla fighters, and weapons capable of hindering the FAS control of the sky. President Reagan was fully aware that without Washington's support the Contra cause was in danger of disappearing, a situation he could not resolve because he was convinced that the existence of Sandinista Nicaragua was a threat to the security of Central America and therefore to that of the United States. In the spring of 1985, he tried to get Congress to reconsider its decision to no longer finance the Contras. In June, he managed to get it to accept $27 million in aid, but only to finance humanitarian equipment in the form of clothing, food and medicines.[1] The President then asked his Administration to continue to support the Contras militarily through the back door.

Since it was no longer possible for the White House to finance this assistance with money from the US budget, the Administration sought private funds and foreign governments. If Israel and South Africa refused, Saudi Arabia agreed in the summer of 1984 to pay $1 million a month to the Contras through a bank in the Cayman Islands.[2] Elliot Abrams, Assistant Secretary of State, even met with the Minister of Defence of the Sultanate of Brunei in London in August 1986, who offered $10 million for the Contras.

Private anti-communist networks were also organizing themselves to supplement the end of US state aid. In May 1984, John Singlaub met with Bill Casey, who informed him that the White House would not oppose private initiatives to support the Contras.[3] After a trip to Costa Rica and Honduras to meet with FDN leaders in the summer of 1984, Singlaub solicited donors in the United States and Europe. He received donations from millionaires such as Ellen Garwood, Nelson Bunker Hunt and Joseph Coors, raising $250,000 in 1984 and 1985. He also obtained about $5 million worth of military equipment from Taiwan and South Korea.[4]

In May 1985, Singlaub began to set up a team of military advisors with the help of Robert K. Brown, the owner of *Soldier of Fortune* magazine. The latter brought together a team called the "Wild Bunch", which included veterans from Vietnam, the fighting in Rhodesia and El Salvador. They settled in Honduras where they trained the Contra fighters. When the camp where they lived was destroyed by a Sandinista rocket attack, the "Wild Bunch" team returned to the United States.[5] Singlaub also set up a modest air force to supply the Contras. These were two C-123K, two C-7A Caribous and a single engine Maule.[6]

Other private organizations, such as the Americare Foundation,

The fin of the ACE C-123K shot down by the Sandinistas near El Tele on 5 October 1986: this incident was to have far-reaching consequences not only for the war in Nicaragua, but also numerous politicians and officials in Washington. (Albert Grandolini Collection)

Freedom's Friends, and the Christian Broadcasting Network supported the Contras by sending significant humanitarian aid.[7] Support also came from Europe. In France, meetings were organised where the public was asked to cover the cost of care for the injured. A Frenchman nicknamed the "Green Jackal", a former paratrooper, was even a military advisor to the FDN.[8] In July 1985, on the border with Nicaragua, Costa Rican authorities arrested five foreign volunteers who had come to fight with the Contras. There were two Americans, two British and one Frenchmen who came to Central America with the help of an Alabama-based group, Civilian Military Assistance.[9] Some activists of the American Indian Movement also travelled to Costa Rica to fight alongside the Miskitos Indians of MISURATA.[10]

In addition to this private aid, Reagan asked the NSC to take over from the CIA and found ways to support the Contras. The NSC, led by Robert McFarlane and Bill Casey, established a secret cell to accomplish this mission, headed by Lt. Colonel Oliver North.[11]

Relying on arms dealers, mercenaries, and former intelligence service operatives, the network set up by North, which was quickly nicknamed "The Enterprise," organized illegal arms purchases to supply the Contras in 1984. Violating numerous US and international laws, North sold weapons, including missiles, to Tehran via Tel Aviv.

Although US law prohibited the supply of weapons to Iran, the Reagan Administration hoped to secure the release of US hostages from Hezbollah in Lebanon. In November 1985, as part of these operations, the Israelis deposited $1 million into an account of The Enterprise in Geneva. North was taking $150,000 of this amount to finance the Contras. He made a new financial transfer in February 1986.[12]

Thanks to the system developed by North and The Enterprise, between $16 million and $25 million of Iranian money was diverted to the Contras.[13] Thus, General Secord, who managed The Enterprise's money, bought 2,200 Egyptian 9mm machine guns in Israel, 5,000 CETME rifles in Spain and 10,000 AKM in Egypt.[14] Supply was provided through two air bases, one in Aguacate, Honduras and the other in Ilopango, El Salvador, both controlled by US agents.[15] It was from these bases that the supply operations for the Contras inside Nicaragua were organized. About 500 such operations were carried out.[16] In 1984, they were executed by the Civilian Military Assistance, a group of US mercenaries who signed contracts with the CIA in conjunction with the US ambassador in Tegucigalpa, John Negroponte. On 1 September, one of the CMA's aircraft was shot down by the Sandinistas, putting an end to the company's activities.[17]

In the spring of 1987, the US channel CBS broadcasted an investigation into the use of drug traffickers' aircraft to resupply the Contras with weapons. In exchange, drug traffickers were allowed to land in the United States with shipments of marijuana and cocaine. The US authorities had always rejected this accusation despite the report of a special Senate subcommittee in 1989 which showed the involvement of the Contras in drug trafficking to the United States.[18]

On 5 October 1986, in southern Nicaragua, an anti-aircraft defence patrol of the BLC Gaspar Garcia Laviana noticed an unmarked C-123K aircraft flying at low altitude near San Carlos. The patrol fired and shot down the aircraft. In the wreckage, EPS soldiers found the bodies of a Nicaraguan and two Americans, while they arrested the crew's only survivor, an American, Eugene Hasenfus.[19] He had served in the US Navy before joining Air America, a CIA-owned company in Southeast Asia. He returned to the United States in 1973 before being contacted by Corporate Air Service in 1986 to fly for ACE and leaving for the Ilopango base in El Salvador.[20] Corporate Air Service and Southern Air Transport belonged to the CIA and were used to supply the Contras, while ACE was a company run by private persons on contract to the CIA. The operations were led by two exiled Cubans; the first was Felix Rodriguez, a veteran of the Bay of Pigs, before advising the Bolivian army on the capture Che Guevara in 1967. Rodriguez then advised the Salvadoran army. He was assisted by Luis Posada

Sandinista troops inspecting the smashed wreckage of the downed C-123K. (Albert Grandolini Collection)

A famous photograph of a handcuffed Hasenfus while escorted away by the group of the Sandinista troops that downed his aircraft. (Albert Grandolini Collection)

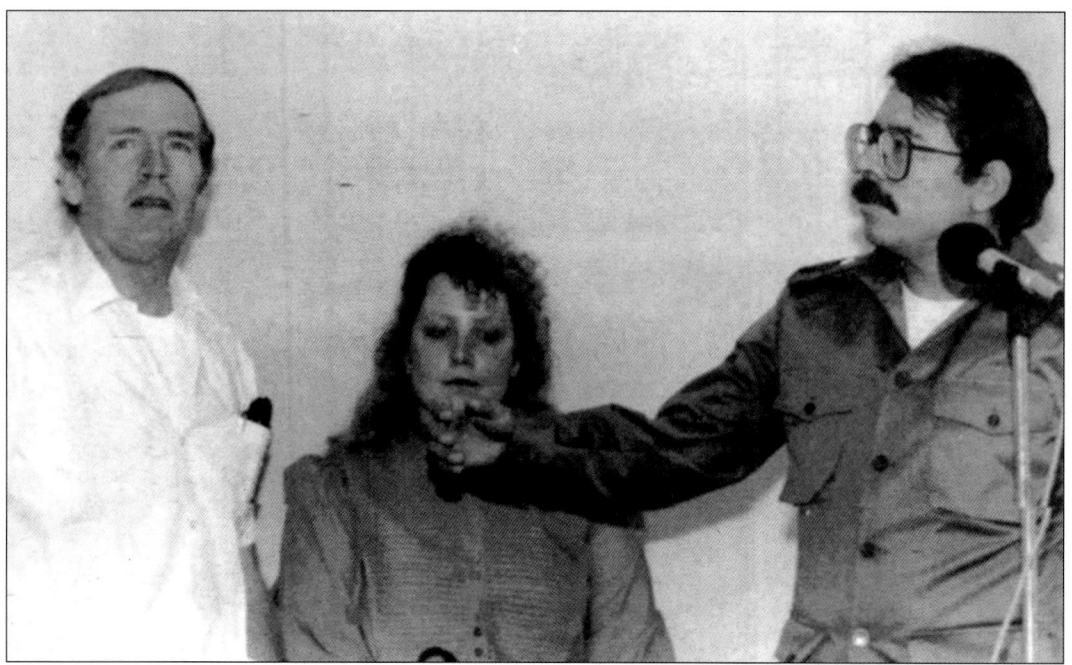

Eugene Hasenfus with his wife and Daniel Ortega, before being returned to the US authorities. While the clandestine involvement of the highest officials in Washington in supporting the Contras was entirely ignored by the US public until that point in time, investigations prompted by the capture of Hasenfus nearly lead to an impeachment of President Ronal Reagan. (Albert Grandolini Collection)

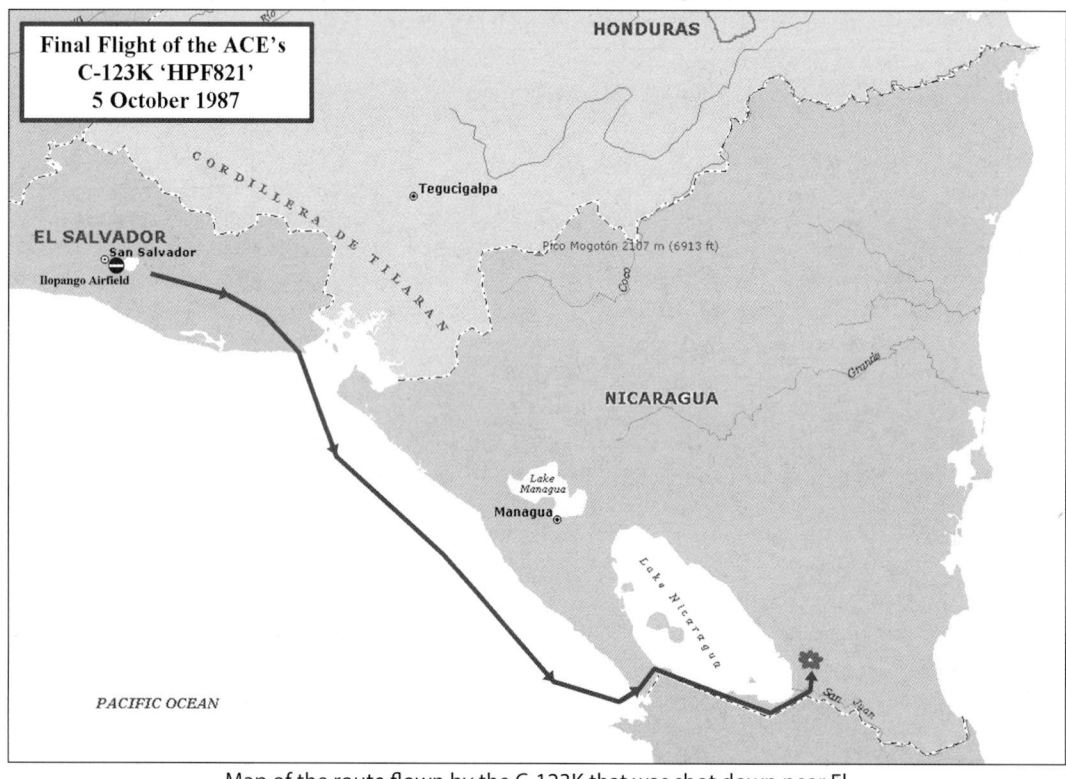

Map of the route flown by the C-123K that was shot down near El Tele on 5 October 1986. (Map by Tom Cooper)

Carriles, also a veteran of the Bay of Pigs before heading to Venezuela where he organized the in-flight explosion of a Cuban commercial aircraft in 1976.[21]

The capture of Hasenfus, which was widely reported by Managua, revealed in the open, the continued US involvement in the civil war in Nicaragua despite the ban passed by Congress.

The Difficult Union of the Contras

In early 1986, the Reagan administration again asked Congress to vote for assistance for the Contras, but the House of Representatives rejected the proposal on 20 March. The situation became more and more critical for the FDN, which then had about 18,000 fighters.[22] The lack of US military assistance was cruelly felt, while the new commander of the Honduran army, General Humberto Regalado and President Azcona were increasingly reluctant to support them. To unblock the situation, Reagan used the armed incursions of the EPS into Honduras to denounce the threat posed by the Sandinista government to neighbouring countries. Under pressure from Washington, the Honduran government requested US military assistance. On 25 March, the Pentagon sent 600 soldiers to the area, while the next day the Senate voted in favour of further aid to the Contras. The House of Representatives had yet to be convinced. To this end, the Reagan administration relied on Arturo Cruz, who joined the Contras leadership in June 1985 in the hope of transforming them into a democratic force. The mirage of this possible reform weakened the hesitant and on June 25, the House of Representatives votes for $100 million in aid.[23]

In early November 1986, a Lebanese newspaper reported that Washington had supplied sophisticated weapons to Iran. Congress then launched an investigation that lasted more than a year and uncovered the secret Contra funding operations conducted by North and the NSC.[24] The "Irangate" scandal was a severe blow to Reagan's Nicaraguan policy, but it came a few months after the vote on the $100 million aid, aid that represented both a breath of fresh air for the Contras and also the last chance to win over the Managua regime.

As Washington resumed its military aid, it was trying to unify the Contras. Since 1984, negotiations had been organized between the various forces opposed to the Sandinistas. In July 1984, negotiations were held in Panama under the aegis of Richard Stone, former Special Ambassador for Latin America, between the FDN and ARDE. An agreement was signed stipulating that the two organizations would fight until the creation of a transitional government and the organization of free elections. They also undertook to coordinate their military and political actions through a common command. But this agreement led to the division of ARDE. If Robelo was in favour, Pastora was strongly opposed. The latter therefore did not recognise the Panama Agreement.[25]

Finally, on 12 June 1985, the Contras announced the formation of the United Opposition of Nicaragua (UNO), which included the FDN, MISURA, Robelo's MDN and Arturo Cruz's Nicaraguan Democratic Coordination.[26] The UNO aimed to oust the Sandinistas from power and establish a democratic Nicaragua. It thus offered a new image of the Contra cause, pluralist and civil, in order to give them more credibility on the international level, particularly with the US Congress.

The UNO was soon hit by divisions. Within it, the FDN was the dominant component since it had the most important military forces, a position that was enhanced by its close ties with the MISURA. Moderate groups led by Cruz and Robelo felt marginalized by the FDN Conservatives, most of whom were former Somoza supporters.[27] This division was also geographical since the UNO Southern Front, which operated from Costa Rica under the command of Fernando Chamorro "El Negro", complained that it did not receive enough aid to lead the fight. A UNO meeting in Miami in May 1986 failed to resolve the conflicts. Despite the intervention of Elliot Abrams, Deputy Secretary of State, Cruz left the organization at the beginning of 1987.[28]

It was on the ruins of the UNO that the Nicaraguan Resistance (RN) was formed in Miami on 7 May 1987.[29] It brought together 54 opposition groups, the main ones being the FDN and the BOS, with a management of seven people. The most important members of this coalition were Adolfo Calero and Aristides Sanchez of the FDN, Alfonso Robelo and Pedro Chamorro of the BOS. In reality, the RN was in the hands of the FDN, which had most of the organizational, financial and military resources.

The Contra Miskistos were also trying to unite. On 27 June 1987, KISAN, MISURA and MISURATA united in a single organization called Yatama, which means "The Descendants of Mother Earth" in the Miskito language.[30] However, this organization was unable to resolve the conflicts that had torn apart Miskito leaders for years, including Rivera and Fagoth.

The US efforts to unify the Contras were part of a particular context. The end of 1986 marked a turning point in the Nicaraguan conflict. Irangate paralysed the Reagan administration, whose operational capacities were weakened in Central America. This situation caused a certain panic in Honduras, which feared to find itself alone in front of the Sandinistas while it sheltered thousands of Contra fighters on its soil. Jose Azcona, the President of Honduras, then pressured them to leave his country as soon as possible.[31] The Contras were aware that the $100 million voted by Congress would be the last major aid coming from Washington and that they only had a few months to turn the situation around and took advantage of the Managua government. In November 1986, UNO leaders met in Costa Rica to determine ways to expand their military operations and increase their support base among the population.[32]

The Last Contra Offensives

In order to intensify their actions and resume the initiative against the EPS, the Contras needed modern weaponry that could only be provided by the US. In November 1986, William Casey met with the FDN direction in Yamales to develop the delivery of M79 grenade launchers, FIM-43C Redeye missiles, 57mm recoilless rifles and weapons of Soviet origin.[33] The logistics of delivering this armament to Honduras was entrusted to General James Hardy and it was from Swan Island on the coast of Honduras or from the Palmerola Military Air Base that CIA pilots carried out more than 300 Contra supply operations inside Nicaragua, at a rate of about three to four per week.[34]

The anti-tank mines provided by the CIA soon covered the roads in the northern regions of the country, causing damage to both EPS and civilian vehicles, such as on 2 July 1986, when a mine killed 33 bus passengers near El Cuá.[35] The roads, strewn with rocks and at times impassable, were vital to both the Sandinista army and the thousands of peasants who live in this poor agricultural zone. Mines thus made it possible to hinder the mobility of the EPS, whose troops had the advantage of moving quickly in East German-made trucks.

The most critical delivery for the Contras was portable ground-to-air missiles such as the SA-7 and FIM-43 Redeye MANPADs, which broke the EPS' advantage in tactical mobility. The Redeye, which could be fired by an individual soldier, was by far the most potent weapon in the Contra arsenal. Its automatic guidance system could deliver a high-explosive warhead to a target up to 5km away. Until then, the only anti-aircraft weapons in the Contras' possession were those taken from their opponents. Thus, the first Sandinista helicopter shot down was a Mi-8 hit on 2 December 1985, near Mulukutu, by a Soviet-made missile taken from the EPS by the Contras.[36]

Better equipped than ever before, the Contras now began bringing down FAS helicopters – some, it was claimed, with help of US-supplied FIM-92A Stinger MANPADs. While the Sandinistas continued to carry out mobile air operations, they were now reluctant to conduct air assault missions or allow helicopters to be parked for long periods of time to provide fire support to ground troops. This situation made the counter-insurgency strategy of the EPS much less effective.[37]

By the end of 1986, equipped with the modern weapons provided by the CIA, the Contras' fighters were once again preparing to infiltrate Nicaragua. Aware that the resumption of US support would revive enemy activity, in early 1987, EPS concentrated about 35,000 soldiers in the north of the country. For its part, the FDN had 15,000 combatants in Honduras while approximately 2,500 maintained a physical presence in the country in small units.

The FDN then launched Operation *Ofensiva de Primavera*, which aimed both at destroying economic and strategic objectives and strengthening military activity in the central and southern parts of the RM 5.[38] CR Jorge Salazar 3 with 700 men was ordered to infiltrate to reach the Chontales area. The purpose of this infiltration was not to fight the Sandinista in the north of the country but to establish a link with the units in the centre of the country. CR Jorge Salazar 3 faced the EPS at Rancho Grande near the Waslala road. The majority of the fighters managed to continue their journey but all the commanders of the Task Forces were killed.[39]

In March, FDN units entered Nicaragua with the intention of attracting the Sandinistas to fight in the mountains north of Jinotega. The operation was one of the most important since the beginning of the war. The Contra forces seized Wina but had to face five BLIs. On the Sandinista side there were more than 3,000 fighters and 36 helicopters under the command Lieut. Col. Manuel Salvatierra.[40] The fighting lasted nearly three months. On 10 May, four helicopters attacked the Contras defending El Cartelón, one of which was shot down by a Redeye missile. However, the EPS seized the FDN airstrips at San Andrés de Bocay using Mi-25 helicopters and BM-21 rocket launchers, though the fighting still continued for many days around the airstrips that were destroyed by the Sandinistas. Finally, the EPS abandoned the area after having mined it, before the 800 Contra fighters returned to Honduras.[41]

Despite, or thanks to, the fighting in the north, the Contras

Tube Missiles

The final phase of the Contra War in Nicaragua was dominated by one kind of armament: the man-portable air defence systems (MANPADs). All of the types that saw combat deployment during the conflict of the 1980s had one thing in common: their missiles were launched from a tube, to which a grip stock and thermal battery were attached. This is why they became known as 'tube missiles'.

The first to become available in Nicaragua – and then on both sides – was the Soviet-made 9K32M Strela-2 (ASCC/NATO-codename 'SA-7b Grail'). Originally envisaged as a battalion-level air defence system, the Strela was based on the design of the US-made FIM-43 Redeye, from which it borrowed heavily, even though it could not be described as a 'reverse engineered copy'. When ready to fire, the grip stock with the tube and missile weighted a total of 15kg (33.1lbs). The SA-7b had a slant range of 4.2km (2.6 miles) and a ceiling of 2.3km (1.43 miles), and a slightly improved seeker head and control logic, although retaining the original, rather problematic warhead with poor lethality of the SA-7a. Following protracted development, it entered service in 1968, and by 1969 found its way into the Egyptian armed forces, where it scored its first operational victory against an Israeli-operated fighter bomber. Like the FIM-43, the SA-7 was an infra-red homing weapon: its seeker head could see energy in the near-infrared spectrum, foremost that exhausted by very hot surfaces inside the jet nozzle. Essentially, this allowed only rear-aspect engagement of jet aircraft or helicopters.

The Sandinistas had received about 100 SA-7s already in 1981, and scored their first kills at least two years later (see Table 7 for details): by the end of the war, at least five aircraft operated on behalf of the Contras had been shot down by the EPS.

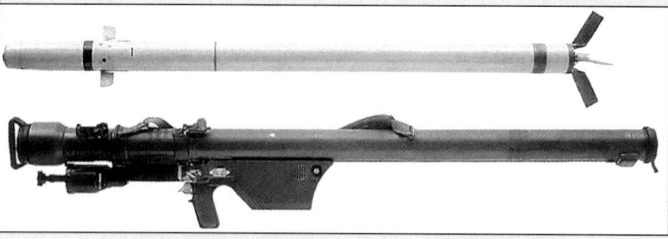

The first MANPADs operated by the Contras were a few SA-7bs captured from the Sandinistas: ultimately, they obtained about 30 rounds in that fashion. Subsequently, the CIA provided them with 80 SA-7bs and trained 15 gunners in their use. However, in 1986 the Contras received an older – though more powerful – weapon: based on research and development run by the US Army since 1948, in 1962 the General Dynamics FIM-43 Redeye was the first infra-red homing MANPAD ever to enter service. Similar to the subsequent SA-7, the Redeye missile is fired from the M171 launcher, including a tube and the grip stock: ready to fire, the entire system weighted 13.3kg (29.3lbs). The operator would visually track the target using a sight until the missile acquired it – and confirmed this by a buzzing signal. The operator then pressed the trigger that fired the initial booster stage and launched the missile out of the tube. At a safe distance (about six metres/seven yards) from the operator, the missile's spring-loaded fins popped out (four stabilizing fins at the rear and two control surfaces at the front) and the sustainer motor ignited, accelerating the missile to its peak velocity of about Mach 1.7. The warhead was armed about 1.25 seconds after the sustainer was ignited. The Redeye had an effective engagement range of up to 4,500m (14,800ft).

Withdrawn from use by the USA in the early 1980s (and

9K32M missile with its grip stock. (US Navy Photo)

ARDE troops assembling a SA-7 grip stock before going to action in 1985. (US DoD)

continued to infiltrate and travelled through central Nicaragua from the Honduran border to the Costa Rican border. They were particularly active in the central part of the country. In June, they launched attacks in the La Esperanza area, in the Rama region, and also in the Chontales region.[42] On 14 July 1987, they attacked San José de Bocay, but were quickly repelled. The Contra forces had now moved into a new stage of the war. Since the beginning of the year, virtually the entire Contra force, as many as 10,000 men or more, had infiltrated successfully into Nicaragua from the bases in Honduras where troops had languished for two years.

The Esquipulas Agreements

Since 1982, the CIA hoped to build a Southern Front as powerful as the Northern Front, but relations with Pastora were complicated as he had always refused to put himself under the total control of the US. The Agency withdrew all supplies and organized the defection of 6 of his main lieutenants. In March 1986, when Pastora definitively abandoned the armed struggle, the BOS, which had gathered ARDE's remains since July 1985, had only 300 fighters.[45] Nevertheless, it carried the CIA's hopes of opening a strong Southern Front. In May 1986, the BOS commanders appointed Fernando Chamorro as head of the military organization. The latter already led the Nicaraguan Democratic Union, a formation close to the UNO, which suggested that the BOS could, with the support of the CIA and in cooperation with the FDN, take on the Sandinista forces.[46]

For its part, Costa Rica, which needed Washington's economic assistance to deal with its economic problems, agreed in the early 1980s to let the CIA use its territory to support the Contras. Thus, in 1985, the CIA, with the consent of the Costa Rican government, built an air base in Santa Elena near the border with Nicaragua. This situation changed in May 1986 with the election of Oscar Arias as President of Costa Rica. The new Costa Rican president called for the Santa Elena air base to be closed. Despite the US threat to stop economic aid to his country, he remained firm and the base was closed in September.

After having defeated the CIA's plan to open a second front, Arias set out to find a solution to the Nicaraguan conflict. He shared

An ARDE operator with a captured SA-7 in 1985. (US DoD)

The Contra gunner that shot down the FAS Mi-17 serial number 282 on 20 September 1987, with a FIM-43C grip stock. (via J. H.)

Chief of Staff FDN, Bermudez with a CIA-supplied FIM-43C in August 1987. (US DoD)

replaced by what was originally the Redeye II, but subsequently named the FIM-92A Stinger), a quantity of the final variant – FIM-43C Block III – was taken over by the CIA and provided to several allies around the World. As far as is known, the ARDE and the FDN received 187: out of the total of 297 MANPADs they had been donated by the CIA or captured from the Sandinistas, 157 were fired in training or in combat, or were captured by the FAS during airdrops that went astray. The Contras claimed a total of 27 kills in 1987 alone, while the FAS confirmed a loss of a total of 17 helicopters lost to all reasons in combat operations between 1979 and 1990, of which 6 crashed for non-combat reasons, and 11 were shot down (5 in 1987), killing 43 crewmembers and 61 passengers (for details, see Table 7 on the next page).[43]

Reports according to which the ARDE and the FDN received the more advanced General Dynamics FIM-92A Stingers remain unconfirmed: supposedly, the CIA assessed the Redeye as 'adequate' because the FAS operated no fixed wing aircraft by this point in the war.[44] The appearance of large numbers of MANPADS in the Contras' arsenal forced the FAS to acquire exhaust diffusers and install these on surviving Mi-8s, Mi-17s, and Mi-25s.

Washington's anti-Sandinism, but was aware that the military solution led to deadlock. He was therefore looking for political ways to stop the hostilities but also to put the Sandinista government in difficulty.

Since the beginning of the conflict, diplomatic efforts had been made to end the war. Contadora's group, European leaders, including Spain's Felipe González, the Secretaries General of the OAS and the UN had sought ways to bring peace to Nicaragua, but all these efforts failed.[47] Managua wanted to negotiate only with Washington so as not to have to recognize the Contras and legitimize them.[48] Upon this request, however, the White House responded that the Sandinistas had to negotiate directly with the Contras. The situation seemed to be blocked and the war looked to continue indefinitely.

Arias' efforts nevertheless had a positive response from the region's heads of state, who were concerned about the intensification of the war in Nicaragua since the resumption of US aid to the Contras. For the President of Guatemala, Vinicio Cerezo "the situation is entering a critical phase. There is a slide toward militarism that could be leading Nicaragua to a tragedy without precedent in the history of Central America."[49]

In February 1987, Arias invited the presidents of Guatemala, El Salvador and Honduras to San José. The four presidents agreed on the principles of a peace process for the region. Each government had to negotiate a ceasefire with the rebels in their countries, declare an amnesty and hold free elections. Above all, they demanded that foreign powers stop supporting the various guerrillas.

To promote the San José plan, Arias visited leaders from different countries in Latin America and Europe. In Washington, he received the support of the Democrats who dominated Congress. The Sandinista government was initially suspicious, but he understood that the plan proposed by Arias could put an end to all aid to the Contras, the only way to defeat them militarily. At the new summit between Central American heads of state in Esquipulas, Guatemala, on 24 and 25 May, Daniel Ortega was now present.[50]

In June 1987, Arias was received at the White House, which was hostile to the Costa Rican president's initiatives and asked him to change his policy. On this point, Arias was in disagreement with Reagan. Nevertheless, on 7 August, the five Central American presidents met again in Guatemala for the Esquipulas II summit.

Table 7: Known, Confirmed, and Claimed Aircraft & Helicopter Losses of the Contra War, 1979-1990					
Date	place	Weapon	Aircraft Type	Notes
10 Nov 1980	Honduras	-	OH-6A	FAS helicopter flown by Ernesto Venus and journalist Carlos Duran Palavisini landed inside Honduras. Crew and occupants subsequently released
?? Mar 1982	Gulf of Fonseca	small arms fire	aircraft	Honduran Air Force aircraft claimed as shot down by Nicaraguan Coast Guard vessel
7 Mar 1982	Honduras	-	C-47	FAS serial number 208; FAS crew including Gustavo Antonio Kiseda and Octavia Barrera defected to Honduras; aircraft returned to Nicaragua a week later
14 Aug 1982	Managua	-	IAI-201	FAS serial number 223; FAS aircraft crashed due to engine failure; crew including Henry Tablada Ruiz and Abdul Sirkin Gomez and 19 passengers killed
9 Dec 1982	San Andres Bay	-	Mi-8T	FAS serial number 265; crashed due to malfunction, killing pilot Eduardo Hurtado and 84 passengers (mostly children)
?? Dec 1982			Mi-8T	FAS helicopter claimed shot down by FDN over northern Nicaragua
?? Jan 1983			Mi-8T	FAS helicopter claimed shot down by FDN over northern Nicaragua
19 Apr 1983	Jalapa	small arms fire	Hughes 500	ARDE aircraft hit by EPS; crew escaped to Honduras
8 Sep 1983	Managua	37mm	Cessna 404	shot down during attack on Sandino IAP, shortly after destroying an abandoned C-47
8 Sep 1983	Rio San Juan	?	T-28?	crashed while withdrawing from attack on Sandino IAP
3 Oct 1983	Matagalpa	SA-7	DC-3	transport carrying supplies; shot down by Sandinista solider Fausto Palacios; four crewmembers captured, one killed
27 Aug 1984	Jinotega or Nueva Segovia	SA-7	C-47	aircraft operated by the CMA and carrying supplies; shot down by Sandinista soldier Fanor Medina Leyton; eight crewmembers killed
28 Aug 1984	Matagalpa	-	Mi-8T	FAS helicopter crashed due to engine failure; crew of three killed
1 Sep 1984		SA-7	C-47	aircraft operated by the CMA and carrying supplies; claimed shot down by the Sandinistas
8 Sep 1984	Santa Clara	37mm	helicopter	Contra aircraft shot down by the Sandinistas, crew of three killed
?? Sep 1984	Jalapa	SA-7	O-2A	Contra aircraft claimed shot down by the Sandinistas
?? Sep 1984	Jalapa	SA-7	Hughes 500	Contra aircraft claimed shot down by the Sandinistas
21 Nov 1984	Pantasma	-	Mi-8T	FAS helicopter collided with mountain, killing Eddie Brent, Ronaldo Fonseca, and nine passengers
1 Dec 1984	Honduras	-	Bell 206	CIA-operated; crashed for unknown reasons
8 Sep 1985	San Juan del Norte	12.7mm	C-47	FAS aircraft damaged by ground fire
2 Dec 1985	Mulukutu	SA-7	Mi-8	FAS serial number 270; shot down by ARDE; Cuban crew of three and 14 commandos killed
23 Dec 1985	Honduras	-	An-2	FAS pilot Lacayo Silva Blanco defected to Honduras
5 Oct 1986	La Flor	SA-7	C-123K	serial 54-679 (c/n 20128); aircraft operated by ACE and shot down by Sandinista soldier José Ferando Canales Alemán; three crewmember killed, loadmaster Eugene Hasenfus captured
16 Jan 1986	San Juan	14.5mm or FIM-43C	Mi-17	FAS serial number 284; made emergency landing; crew of three OK; claimed shot down by ARDE
16 Jan 1986	San Juan	14.5mm or FIM-43C	Mi-17	FAS serial number 287; damaged by ground fire; crew of three OK; claimed shot down by ARDE
19 Jul 1986	Bluefields	-	Mi-8T	FAS serial number 269; sudden loss of control; eight military personnel and 14 civilians killed; navigator Roberto Chamorro Martinez survived
6 Sep 1986	Cerro Koperno	SA-7	C-47	FAS aircraft shot down by FAS MANPAD; 28 of crew and passengers killed
17 Sep 1986	Jinotega	-	Mi-17	FAS serial number 302; collided with the ground; crew of three killed
30 Oct 1986	Jinotega	-	Mi-17	FAS serial number 294; collided with the ground; 22 crewmembers and passengers killed, navigator and one passenger survived

Date	Location	Weapon	Aircraft	Details
4 Nov 1986		-	Mi-17	FAS serial number 293; crashed, crew of three injured
19 Dec 1986	Managua	-	An-2	FAS serial number 77; collided with the ground; 11 of crew and passengers killed
25 Jan 1987	Nueava Guinea	-	Mi-17	FAS serial number 301; crashed due to engine failure; crew of three injured
5 Mar 1987	El Cartelón	FIM-43C	Mi-25	claimed shot down by the Contras; no loss known to have occurred at this time
15 Apr 1987	Managua	-	An-2	crashed due to engine failure on take-off from Sandino IAP; one killed and nine injured
12 Jun 1987	Jinotega	FIM-43C	Mi-17	FAS serial number 287; the crew of three and 12 passengers killed
19 June 1987	Jinotega	FIM-43C	Mi-25	shot down by the Contras (first Mi-25 loss); crew of three killed
27 Aug 1987	Jinotega	FIM-43C	Mi-17	FAS serial number 307; shot down by the Contras; six out of three crew and 18 passengers killed
20 Sep 1987		FIM-43C	Mi-17	FAS serial number 282; shot down by ARDE; crew of three survived
25 Sep 1987	Matagalpa	FIM-43C	Mi-25	shot down by the Contras (second Mi-25 loss); crew of two killed
11 Oct 1987	Villa Sandino	FIM-43C	Mi-17	FAS serial number 305; shot down by the Contras; two of crew survived, one killed
14 Oct 1987	Villa Sandino	-	Mi-17	FAS serial number 316; crashed for unknown reasons; one killed and two survived
17 Oct 1987	San Rafael del Norte	-	An-2	FAS aircraft caught fire and crashed, killing the crew of two
29 Oct 1987	Nueva Segovia	SA-7	Mi-8T	FAS serial number 281; shot down by FAS troops, six of crew and passengers killed
22 Nov 1987	Costa Rica	-	An-2	FAS serial number 78; crew Carlos Gade Arostegui and Jasinto Ramirez Mendoza defected to Costa Rica
9 Dec 1987	San Huan del Norte	small arms fire	Cessna 152	civilian aircraft shot down by small arms fire; pilot Giordano Denbi captured
?? 1987		SA-7	C-47	Contra aircraft shot down by the Sandinistas, crew of 7 killed, pilot escaped to Honduras
1 Jan 1988	Matagalpa	-	Mi-17	FAS helicopter collided with high tension wires and crashed; one passenger killed; crew of three and 11 soldiers injured
14 Feb 1988	Las Brisas	-	Mi-17	FAS helicopter crashed due to technical malfunction, killing the crew of three
17 Mar 1988	Rio Coco	-	Mi-25	FAS serial 341; main rotor blade and fuselage damaged in attack by FAH SMB.2; no injuries
19 May 1988	Managua	-	Mi-25	FAS helicopter crashed during an exercise; two killed, one injured
8 Dec 1988	Honduras	-	Mi-25	FAS serial number 355; Edwin Estrada Leiva defected to Honduras; helicopter returned about a year later
24 Apr 1989	Costa Rica	-	Cessna 180	FAS registration YN-GBP; Antonio Aranda Gaido defected to Costa Rica
27 Jun 1990	San Pedro de Lovago	-	2 x Mi-17	FAS helicopters collided; 14 injured

They signed a peace process agreement based on freedom of expression for all political parties, freedom of the press, elections under the control of the OAS and the United Nations, the opening of a dialogue with the opposition, the declaration of an amnesty and the opening of negotiations for a ceasefire. Each country also had to set up a National Reconciliation Commission, which included a representative of the government, an opposition representative, a bishop and an independent chosen by the President. While for the Sandinistas this agreement meant the establishment of a "bourgeois democracy" in their country, it had the advantage of leading to the defeat of the Contras since it prohibited the use of the territories of the signatory countries by irregular rebel forces and officially asked the US government to stop all aid to the Contras. For Ortega, signing the agreement was also a way to give legitimacy to his government and, on the contrary, to make the Contras responsible for the conflict.[51]

But when Ortega returned to Managua, he had to face hostility from the rest of the FSLN National Directorate. The discussion was keen and finally the President of Nicaragua went Cuba to get Castro's opinion on the Esquipulas agreement. For Fidel, the latter made it possible to obtain the means to overcome the Contras and had to be accepted by the FSLN.[52]

The Sandinistas were indeed aware that most of the power of the Contras was based on US aid. The Esquipulas Agreement thus opened the prospect of ending Washington's funding of the Contras and being able to resume the military initiative. In the summer of 1987, however, there was still a major obstacle to this hope, the firm rejection of the Esquipulas Agreement by President Reagan.[53]

Washington did not recognize the validity of this agreement and continued to call on Nicaragua to hold free elections within a short period of time under international supervision, or risk continued funding of the Contras. On 8 August, the day after the agreement was signed, Reagan declared that he needed new negotiations before it could be accepted.

On 10 September, Secretary of State Schultz announced that the administration was asking Congress for another $270 million in assistance for the Contras, angering the Central American presidents. While the Sandinista government formed a reconciliation commission chaired by Cardinal Obando and announced that *La Prensa*, the main opposition newspaper, was once again authorized, Reagan's intransigence appeared to be a threat to the peace process. To support Arias and weaken the US position, the Costa Rican President's supporters in Latin America and Europe campaigned hard for him to win the Nobel Peace Prize, which he received on 13 October 1987.

However, the peace process advanced slowly. The Sandinista government called a unilateral ceasefire in three areas of Nicaragua where the Contras were concentrated (Nueva Guinea region, Jinotega and Nueva Segovia departments) to encourage them to lay down their arms.[54] But Honduras, for its part, did nothing to close the camps on its territory, which remained a sanctuary from which the Contras could mount their actions. The fighting went on and intensified as hopes for peace increased.

Operations *David* and *Olivero*

During 1987, the presence of the Contras in the centre of the country continued to increase. In the eastern sections of Matagalpa, Boaco and Chontales provinces, they managed to establish themselves almost permanently and intensified their actions. In September 1987, there were 481 clashes in Nicaragua, killing 416 Contras and 126 Sandinistas.[55]

In October, the Contras launched a large-scale action, Operation *David*, to demonstrate that they had recovered their power. It consisted of a series of mutually supported attacks on the road to Rama, led by the 5,000 fighters of CRs Jorge Salazar 1, 2, 3, 4 and 5, under the direction of Commander Juan Ramon Rivas "Quiché." Its objective was to cut the only improved road linking the Atlantic and Pacific coasts by destroying a key bridge. To support and intensify the impact of the main attack, the Contras also targeted other smaller bridges and also the EPS brigade HQ in Santo Tomás. The units advanced from different locations within RAAS, from the departments of Boaco, Chontales, Jinotega and Matagalpa to the goal of 60km of the Juigalpa-El Rama road.[56] They seized Santo Tomás, La Gateada, Muelle de Los Bueyes and San Pedro de Lóvago, but they failed to destroy the key bridge. They inflicted heavy losses on the Sandinistas, as the EPS lost a thousand men and three helicopters — including a Mi-25 piloted by Fredy Velásquez, the best pilot of the FAS — and a convoy of 18 trucks at the entrance of Cuapa.[57] Operation *David* marked a turning point as the Contras demonstrated their ability to coordinate significant forces to carry out mutually supportive actions. This was the beginning of the transition from a guerrilla strategy to a semi-conventional warfare strategy.

In December of the same year, the Contras once again attempted a large-scale operation, Operation *Olivero*, whose objective was to strike the mining triangle of Sunia, Bonanza and Rosita, an area of strategic importance since the government built a road there that linked the Pacific coast to the port of Puerto Cabezas. The operation also targeted an important EPS unit who protected four military radars that prevented any air resupply of the Contras and which would take three to six months to repair. It also included the runways of an aerodrome, hangars storing Sandinista command equipment in the Atlantic zone and fuel depots.[58]

For this operation, the FDN gathered 7,000 men from 27 Task Forces and 11 CRs in the Las Minas area. Mobilisation and march orders were transmitted to all Task Forces scattered throughout the country, while radio messages were intended to mislead EPS leaders about the real objective of the attack. The latter were convinced that it would take place on the Juigalpa-El Rama road as in Operation *David*.

The fighters already present in Nicaragua moved for 6 weeks from

No way forward: losing all official and clandestine support from Washington, the Contras rapidly found themselves in a precarious position. By early 1988, it became obvious that they could not win the war in Nicaragua, regardless of their relative success on the battlefield or what kind of pressure the USA exercised upon the government in Managua. This column of Contras was photographed while waiting for a signal to continue its march. (Albert Grandolini Collection)

the south of the Chontales and Rama regions. Luis Moreno, along with 600 men from CR Nicarao, was heading towards Siuna during a multi-week march through the mountains and jungle of the country. Commander Tirso Moreno "Rigoberto" and his fighters and men from CR San Jacinto commanded by *Commandante* "Buitre" arrived from the south to meet CR Nicarao on 17 December. The 150 fighters of CR San Jacinto headed southeast and arrived at the Bonanza hydroelectric power plant. The troops commanded by Francisco Ruiz Castellon "Renato" walked southeast towards Rosita and Bonanza. On 14 December 1987, they split up in Rosita and the men of "Renato" took up position in Bonanza. The troops of CR Jorge Salazar 1 went to Siuna, while CR Jorge Salazar 3 reached Rosita on the road linking the mining triangle to Puerto Cabezas.

On 20 December at 5 a.m., the surprise attack began with the taking of Siuna and the destruction of the EPS facilities. *Commandante* "Buitre" and his men destroyed the hydroelectric power plant. Francisco Ruiz Castellon attacked Bonanza and destroyed the military and local State Security installations as well as the mining installations and a power plant in the north of the city. CR Jorge Salazar approached Rosita and occupied nearby roads to block EPS reinforcements.

The attack, carried out by approximately 4,800 fighters, was a complete surprise for the EPS, which failed to detect the opponent's movements, as the latter had benefited from widespread complicity among the population.[59] The Sandinista forces responded by bombarding the villages occupied by the Contras from AN-26 aircraft.

Then, reinforcements from Guaslala, Mulukuku and Puerto Cabezas were ambushed and a T-55 tank was destroyed. The intervention of three Mi-17 helicopters that prevented the Contras from entering Rosita.[60]

Operation *Olivero* was a success. FDN forces seized Siuna and Bonanza for a day and destroyed the surveillance radar base, military garrison facilities, fuel storage and ground support equipment at the aerodrome, portions of two hydroelectric power plants and, most importantly, the RM 5 weapons depot where they seized a thousand AK-47s, a rocket launcher and machine gun system.[61] In this operation they suffered 57 dead and 78 wounded.[62]

Olivero was by far the greatest military success in the conflict against the Sandinista government. While it attracted the world's attention, in the long term it had little effect, as the Contras could not afford to build on this success. The signing of the Esquipulas Treaty and the scale of the Irangate scandal quickly led the Reagan Administration to abandon any hope that Congress would vote for new military aid. This decision disrupted the growth of the Contras forces and prevented them from carrying out larger operations due to the significant logistics they required.

Operation *Danto 88*

At the end of 1987, the RN leaders were aware of the military impasse they were facing due to a lack of US aid. Like the Sandinistas, some wanted to use the Esquipulas agreement to find a political way out of this situation. On 16 September, they met in Guatemala City to form a negotiating committee that included commanders Walter Calderón "Toño" and Diogenes Hernandez "Fernando." In the Atlantic region, where the Miskito resistance was gradually disintegrating (in 1988 there were only 1,500 active fighters and 1,300 at rest) a faction of KISAN opted for negotiation with Managua and leader Uriel Vanegas even signed a peace agreement in October 1987.[63]

On 31 October, Daniel Ortega went to Moscow to meet Gorbachev, who asked him to reach an agreement with the Contras to bring peace to Nicaragua. Back in Managua, Ortega announced on 5 November that Cardinal Obando would act as an intermediary between the government and the Contras' leaders. He then travelled to Washington to meet with Democratic leaders and persuaded them that Nicaragua was moving towards peace. Above all, he wanted to prevent the House of Representatives from voting on the $270 million in aid to the Contras requested by the Reagan Administration.

Talks with the Contras' leaders began in Santo Domingo, Dominican Republic on 3 December, but the intransigence of the Sandinistas blocked the situation. Nevertheless, in January 1988, after a new summit of Central American presidents in Costa Rica, Ortega took a new step forward and announced the end of the state of emergency. On 3 February, the House of Representatives definitively rejected the request for assistance for the Contras. Despite these advances, the peace process stalled due to the Sandinista refusal to grant political reforms. Soon, the government announced that it no longer wanted Obando to act as an intermediary with the Contras.[64] In place of the clergyman, Daniel Ortega appointed his brother, Humberto, as Minister of Defense. This hardening of Managua's position was explained by the desire to start negotiations in a position of strength, which necessarily required a military success.

Since the beginning of 1988, fighting had been sporadic and concentrated in the departments of Jinotega and Matagalpa, where Contra forces made incursions before returning to Honduras for supplies. The end of US aid forced many units to take refuge in Honduras, in the camp complex in the Bocay Valley, after the Tegucigalpa government asked them to leave the Yamales area. These

Walter Calderón – a.k.a. *Commandante* Toño – was one of two chief Contra negotiators with the Sandinista government in 1988. (Albert Grandolini Collection)

camps around San Andres de Bocay were located just across the Rio Coco that formed the border, and appeared to be easy targets for the EPS to strike. The Sandinista General Staff then decided to conduct a major operation with the intention of annihilating them, Operation *Danto 88*, led by Javier Carrión.

At the end of February, Sandinista troops concentrated about 50km from the border, where the EPS command post was located. At the beginning of March, infantry and artillery units (4,500 men, nine transport helicopters, and AN-26s converted into bombers) were gathered in the Bocay region. The EPS was setting up two battle groups. The first was formed with the BLIs Rufo Marin, Santos Lopez, Juan Pablo Umanzor, Francisco Estrada and a reserve infantry battalion. The second included the BLIs Juan Gregorio Colindres, Simon Bolivar, the permanent infantry battalions 73 and 4009 and a reserve infantry battalion. These units were supported by an artillery group, a FAS detachment, and naval and engineering detachments.

At dawn on 1 March, the FAS-DAA carried out a bombardment of the main Contra camp and then the No. 1 group advanced in the direction of Amaka, Santa Rita and Panka Dakura. Group No. 2 progressed along the right flank towards Amaka, Cerro la Coneja, San Andrés de Amaywas. The two groups' objectives were to seize the main Contra camps in Honduran territory. Ground artillery support was provided with 107mm and Grad 1P rocket launchers, 82mm mortars and 57mm guns.[65]

Sandinista units began to test the Contra defences while the FAS bombarded the upper Bocay Valley.[66] One of *Danto 88*'s targets was to destroy the airstrip built by the Contras near the Bocay River. On 9 March, FAS helicopters flying at low altitude approached the border. About 500 soldiers were landed about 10km from the Bocay and Amaka Rivers. The next day, they attacked the airstrip after crossing the Rio Coco. The EPS finally took over the airstrip and completely controlled the Bocay Valley.

Elsewhere, other infantry, artillery, rocket and bombing attacks were ongoing. The Contras retreated while trying to defend their last positions in Nicaragua, including La Coneja Hill, but they had to cross the border. The bombardments of their camps by FAS caused the destruction of stocks of weapons and food.[67] The Sandinistas then penetrated a few kilometres into Honduras through the jungle, but without reaching the main Contra camps, and then quickly withdrew.

The culmination of Operation *Danto 88* took place on 15 March when 5,000 soldiers crossed the border to attack the Contra camps. About 1,500 other soldiers infiltrated deeper to cut off the enemy's retreat and set up behind the San Andrés de Bocay base. The Contras, about 1,500 of them, tried to defend their position on the border but when they retreated, they found themselves surrounded. The fighting continued on the 17th, but the President of Honduras asked Ortega to withdraw his forces while Honduran aircraft, Super Mystère B.2, A-37s, and Casa C-101s conducted two bombing raids against the Sandinistas. Humberto Ortega finally ordered the bulk of his forces to withdraw from Honduras. However, a few units remained on the scene until the 19th, leading to

Although operating under increasing threat from MANPADs, FAS helicopters continued playing the crucial role on the battlefield, through enabling the EPS to outmatch the mobility of the Contras. During Operation *Danto 88*, they quickly deployed the Sandinista troops around the enemy flanks and into their rear – already well inside Honduras. (Albert Grandolini Collection)

A pair of Mi-17s in the process of deploying troops on a selected landing zone during Operation *Danto 88*. Notable in this photograph is not only the armament consisting of UB-32-57 rocket pods and the UPK-23 gun pods (containing 23mm twin-barrel cannon), but also the 12.7mm machine gun installed in the nose: this was fired by the third crewmember from a position between the pilot and co-pilot/navigator. (Albert Grandolini Collection)

further bombardments by Honduran aircraft. The Contra losses were severe but the EPS had failed to capture the opponent's main base or eradicate the Contra infrastructure.[68]

While Operation *Danto 88* was a military success for the Sandinistas, with the destruction of logistical bases and medical facilities, its political cost was significant. Washington responded by increasing military aid to Honduras and sending 3,200 troops to the Palmerola base in central Honduras.[69] There was a great risk that *Danto 88* would also trigger the vote for new US military aid to the Contras, while Moscow took the opportunity to drop Managua. The military gain of such an operation no longer justified its political cost.

Danto 88 also revealed to the leaders of the RN the tenuousness of their situation. The Contras, without US assistance, were indeed unable to launch a counter-offensive. They had lost their bases in the Bocay Valley and were facing well-equipped Sandinista troops ready to resume the offensive.[70] The search for an agreement with the Managua government then appeared to be the best solution to avoid total defeat.

8
THE LONG ROAD TO PEACE (1988-1990)

Following Operation *Danto 88*, the Contras no longer posed a serious military threat to the Sandinistas' power. Nevertheless, the latter continued negotiations with their opponents even if it was now in a position of strength. This political orientation was explained by the Sandinista defeat on the economic level.

The Economic Collapse of Nicaragua

While the first months of Sandinista rule were marked by an economic upturn, the situation deteriorated rapidly and continued to deteriorate during the 1980s. The external debt, which was $1,600 million in 1979, reached $7,220 million in 1988. It was explained by the ever-increasing military spending, the launch of pharaonic projects without results, and the collapse of the Cordobas' exchange rate. While the economy had been seriously affected by pressure from the United States, it had also been seriously affected by many measures adopted by the government. Thus, due to an increasingly overvalued exchange rate by the government, exports had steadily declined.

The food subsidy system quickly became unmanageable when inflation widened the gap between producer and consumer prices, causing the budget deficit to reach intolerable levels. Production declined almost continuously and real GDP per capita in 1988 returned to the level of the 1950s, the lowest in Central America. To address this situation, the government took measures such as banning street vending. The authorities also erected roadblocks to prevent the unauthorized transport of agricultural products to cities. The objective was to make the State, through the Ministry of Internal Trade, the power that controlled production and prices. To regulate distribution, State stores were set up. In the countryside, farmers were pushed to organize cooperatives to benefit from seeds and fertilizers. The mistrust that developed between producers, traders and the authorities quickly led to a shortage and the introduction of ration cards.

High inflation rates and official controls on production and distribution promoted black market growth while unemployment increased and wages stagnated. The few consumer goods imported by the State were distributed to Sandinista members of trade unions, peasant organizations and the CDS at preferential prices. In reality, many of these products were diverted, resulting in increased shortages, queues and public dissatisfaction.

The economic aid provided by Moscow and the socialist bloc prevented a collapse of the country's economy, but in 1987 Mikhail Gorbachev decided to reduce this aid.[1] This marked the beginning of the Sandinista regime's most severe economic crisis. Trade relations with the Soviet bloc had not been successful and Nicaragua's historical economic dependence had not been resolved. The Sandinistas only replaced US aid with that of the USSR, without the latter ever being able to cover the losses caused by the breakdown of relations with the United States, and Nicaragua could not turn to the IMF, the World Bank and the Inter-American Development Bank to get out of the crisis, as Washington vetoed loans to Managua.[2] The mobilization of international solidarity organizations, particularly left-wing ones, in favour of Nicaragua were unable to restore the situation. It was not until 1988 that the FSLN attempted to change its economic policy by appointing Alejandro Martínez Cuenca as Minister of Planning. The latter accepted the IMF's proposal to send a mission to put forward an economic adjustment plan. This plan included a currency change to curb inflation, strict control of public spending and a consolidation of credit institutions.[3] But the FSLN did not want to reduce the budgets of the army and police until the danger of the Contras was definitively eliminated, which caused the failure of the Cuenca plan. To complicate matters, in October 1988, the country was hit by Hurricane Joan, which caused immense damage, and then by a severe drought in 1989. Peace then became a necessity to save the country from complete bankruptcy.

The Sapoá Agreement

Negotiations between the RN and the Sandinistas continued in San José in January 1988 and Guatemala City in February. During these negotiations, Miskitos leaders also participated, including a member of the Council of Elders, Anciano Cletan Mitchel and the Chief of Staff of KISAN, Osorno Coleman "Comandante Blas."[4] At the same time, the government negotiated with the opposition political parties to oversee the implementation of the Esquipulas agreements and agreed on the pace of liberalization of the regime.

In March 1988, contacts between the Sandinistas and the Contras increased. The government proposed direct negotiations in Sapoá near the border with Costa Rica and the Contras' leaders accepted. Negotiations began on March 21, and on 23 March, under the aegis of the OAS Secretary General, Daniel Ortega and Adolfo Calero signed a peace agreement. It established a 60-day truce from 1 April 1988 to negotiate a final ceasefire.

The Sandinista government agreed to establish freedom of the press, invited the exiles to return and released all political prisoners, including the former GNs. The Contras agreed to recognize the legitimacy of the government, to gather their fighters in special areas, to lay down their arms and to no longer receive assistance from the United States.[5] This aid had become increasingly precarious since the break-up of Irangate; Congress was no longer interested and Bernie

In one of the final acts of the Contra War, on 8 December 1988, the FAS pilot Edwin Estrada Leiva flew this Mi-25 to Honduras, to request political asylum. The helicopter was returned to Nicaragua about a year later. (Albert Grandolini Collection)

Aronson, the new Under-Secretary of State for American Affairs, announced to the Contras that Washington had ceased its military support to help only the civilian political opposition.[6]

Despite the signing of the Sapoá Treaty, peace was difficult to establish. The agreement led to discontent within the RN, which was divided between Calero's supporters who were in favour of ending the fighting and Bermudez's supporters who wanted to continue. The C-in-C was suspicious of the civilian leaders of the RN, whom he suspected of wanting to give priority above all to their future political careers. Bermudez also had to face the slingshot of regional commanders who challenged his leadership and fighters and commanders on the ground had always criticized the easy and sometimes sumptuous lives of staff leaders. They believed that their refusal to lay down their arms was more a sign of their willingness to continue to enjoy a good life than motivated by ideological reasons.[7] The majority of the commanders led by Encarnacion Valdivia "Tigrillo" requested Bermudez's dismissal, thus supporting Calero's solution.[8] This dissent had an impact on the Contra forces that remained within the country. In July, Commander "Dumas", who led the powerful CR Jorge Salazar 5, abandoned Nicaragua due to the lack of ammunition.[9]

The Honduran authorities, at the CIA's request, intervened and decided to expel Bermudez's opponents. The latter with the CR Jorge Salazar 5 and the men of the *Comando de Operacionas Tacticas* settled in the Yamales area and set up roadblocks on the Yamales-Capire road. The Honduran army then issued an ultimatum to the dissidents, and the rebel commanders left for Miami. Bermudez and opponents to the Sapoá agreements took over the leadership of the RN but the commanders of the Southern Front soon demanded Bermudez's withdrawal. They obtained the dissolution of Bermudez's staff in December, then, in February 1989, the assembly of commanders dismissed Bermudez and replaced him with Juan Ramon Rivas "Quiché" and then Israel Galeano "Franklin."[10]

Bermudez's departure did not mean the surrender of the Contras. They refused to lay down their arms until they had firm guarantees for political reforms. Inside Nicaragua, where 500 FDN fighters still lived,

fighting continued. Major Xavier Hidalgo, one of the best Sandinista specialists in the fight against counter-insurgency, was killed near Chontales, while between April 1988 and September 1989, some 230 FDN fighters were killed.[11]

On their side, the Sandinistas still violently repressed rallies by opponents, as in Nandaime on 10 July 1988.[12] The EPS designed the "Camilo and Augusto C. Sandino" plan, which improved the country's defence system by massively organizing the population to participate in national defence in accordance with the principles of the "national patriotic and popular war" and the irregular combat units, BLIs and BLCs, were thus reorganized into tactical combat groups. The aim was to ensure border control and security of the main economic structures.

Despite many failures, the truce signed in Sapoá was extended for more than 18 months while actions by the Contras became rare by the end of 1989. The Sandinistas and RN military leaders met regularly in Managua to set the conditions for the disarmament of troops.[13]

On the political level, in September 1988 the Law on the Regional Autonomy of the Atlantic Coast was approved, while in October the Law on Political Parties was amended to allow for a greater focus on opposition parties. On 17 March 1989, the government released nearly 2,000 former GNs from jail. In the following months, it continued to liberalize the regime, notably in April by adopting a new electoral law that allowed equal access to the media, the right to receive external funding and the right to invite international observer missions. On 14 February 1989, at a new meeting of Central American heads of state, Daniel Ortega announced the organization of elections in Nicaragua on 25 February 1990 under the supervision of a UN observation mission. For his part, the President of Honduras promised to demobilize the Contras.

The upheavals of 1989 contributed to the acceleration of the peace process in Nicaragua. Reagan's departure was a cause for satisfaction for the Sandinistas, who lost their greatest adversary, while the new US President, George Bush, was more concerned about events in Eastern Europe that were leading to the end of the Cold War. The Bush Administration therefore sought a political and diplomatic path to end the conflict in Nicaragua and on 24 March 1989, it decided to support the Esquipulas Treaty.[14] Above all, US officials were aware of the military failure of the Contras. Elliott Abrams thus admitted at the end of 1988 that "the insurgents are finished as a military force."[15] But the disappearance of the Eastern Bloc and the Soviet decision to no longer support revolutionary movements also meant that Managua lost powerful allies and Ortega admitted that Nicaragua could not fight against the direction of history.[16]

In August 1989, the Tela agreements between the Contras and Sandinistas were signed in Honduras. It provided for the demobilization and repatriation of Contra combatants, a process to be carried out under the aegis of an International Support and Verification Commission led by the Secretaries-General of the United Nations and the OAS. On the military side, Security Council Resolution 644 created the United Nations Observer Group in Central America (ONUCA), composed of unarmed soldiers from Argentina, Brazil, Canada, Colombia, Ecuador, India, Ireland, Sweden, Venezuela and Spain, to ensure that the Contras no longer received foreign aid.

From the summer of 1989, without any further hope of receiving US aid, the Contra forces in Honduras moved closer to the border. From October onwards, they decided to enter Nicaragua in order to put pressure on the results of the presidential elections of February 1990 and also to be able to negotiate the demobilisation process in a position of force. They settled around Esteli, Matagalpa, La Trinidad, Juigalpa and low-intensity fighting against the EPS continued into early 1990.[17]

On the economic level, the situation in Nicaragua was desperate. At the beginning of 1989, inflation was above 100% per month and the Sandinistas were faced with the prospect of a complete collapse of the monetary and financial system. Orthodox measures to curb inflation were no longer possible to avoid and the government began to fire thousands of public sector workers, including members of the armed forces, risking its chances in the 1990 presidential elections.

To face these elections, the anti-Sandinista opposition gathered in April 1989 in the Unión Nacional Opositora (UNO, National Opposition Union) and chose Violeta Chamorro as its candidate.[18] On the Sandinista side, the candidate was Daniel Ortega. The FSLN was convinced that it would win and therefore accepted that the election would be held under the aegis of the UN and the OAS and with full freedom of expression and assembly. For the Sandinistas, a victory in free elections was the best way to ensure their legitimacy both domestically and internationally. To everyone's surprise, on 25 February, Violeta Chamorro won with 55% of the votes against Daniel Ortega, who accepted his defeat, with 42% of the vote.[19] In the countryside, the central and Atlantic regions voted for the opposition while the cities and the Pacific region chose the Sandinistas. Violeta Chamorro's victory, which marked the end of the last revolutionary utopia of the 20th century, expressed above all the strong desire for peace that existed among the population.

A Difficult Demobilization

A few days after the electoral victory of Violeta Chamorro, the RN came into contact with the new power to initiate the demobilization process. In the following months, the new Nicaraguan government initiated a reconstruction program that included the demobilization of Contras and the gradual reduction of EPS forces. The Toncontin agreement between the Chamorro government, and the RN asked the UN that ONUCA oversaw the demobilization of the Contras which was due to be completed on 20 April.

On 18 April 1990, a new ceasefire signed between the government and the RN specified the organization of demobilization zones inside

Sandinista troops with a captured FIM-43 Redeye MANPAD in October 1987. (EPS)

Nicaragua where the Contras were to gather and hand over their weapons, which were to be destroyed. All these operations were carried out under the supervision of ONUCA, which was reinforced by UN peacekeepers. Each fighter who had laid down his weapons received a UN certificate attesting to his demobilization. On 6 July, the operation ended. More than 22,000 Contras were disarmed and demobilized, the majority in Nicaragua, the rest in the Honduran camps, 70 tons of military equipment were also destroyed. A programme to reintegrate the former Contras into civilian life had been set up, including the granting of agricultural land. On 27 June, the RN staff under the leadership of Israel Galeano laid down their weapons to officially end the war that had been ravaging the country for a decade.[20]

On the EPS side, from 1991 to 1993, 25,500 professional soldiers were demobilized and nearly 50,000 conscripts returned home, reducing the EPS from 96,000 to 28,000 and then to 14,500 in 1996.[21] In 1994, the EPS became the Nicaraguan Army (*Ejercito Nacional*) over which the Sandinistas lost control while Cuban and Russian influence was eliminated.[22] The army became a professional and non-partisan institution subordinate to the civilian power. Its participation in humanitarian missions, particularly during natural disasters such as Hurricane Mitch in 1998, gave it great legitimacy among the population. It was also at this time that it resumed cooperation with the US military, especially in the fight against drug trafficking, and in 2003, a small contingent was sent to Iraq alongside US forces.[23]

In a country facing many economic difficulties, the return to civilian life for Contras fighters was nevertheless difficult, especially since many of the promises made by the government had not been followed up. Some ex-Contras did not hesitate to take up arms again. In October 1990, 200 *Recontras*, as they were called, seized Waslala, and in November of the same year, a police station in Jalapa. They coordinated within the *Frente Democratico de Salvacion Nacional* (National Salvation Democratic Front) or *Frente Norte 3-80* to protest against the poor conditions of their reintegration into civilian life. In reaction to their actions, demobilized members of the EPS also took up arms, as the *Recompas* that were structured in the *Movimiento de Autodefensa Nacional* (Self-defence National Movement) or the *Frente Obrero y Campesino* (Workers and Peasants Front), which held an area north of Esteli. In 1992, there were nearly 22,000 *Recompas* and *Recontras* in Nicaragua, but they only carried out occasional and sporadic actions. *Recompas* and *Recontras* sometimes united to become *Revueltos*. These groups were gradually falling into banditry, in particular by extorting "war taxes" and prolonging a climate of insecurity in the regions where they operated. The crisis intensified in 1993 when *Recontras* took 38 people hostage to demand the resignation of Humberto Ortega, the head of the EPS. Finally, the hostages were released and Ortega resigned from his position in February 1995. From 1990 to 1995, Nicaragua experienced more than 1,500 armed clashes, particularly in the northern departments but gradually the *Recompas*, *Recontras* and *Revueltos* groups disappeared.[24]

The Difficult Learning of Democracy

Violeta Chamorro's presidency was an era of disillusionment. The Contras' leaders were excluded from the new power while ordinary combatants had difficulty reintegrating into civilian life. On the EPS side, thousands of military personnel were dismissed without compensation, as were 5,000 MINT officials. Neoliberal economic policy increased poverty and unemployment without bringing in enough foreign exchange to finance the demilitarization of the country. For its part, the FSLN became an opposition party but affected by Daniel Ortega's corruption and authoritarianism, internal opponents left it to found the Sandinista Refoundation Movement in 1995, which brought together historical figures of Sandinism such as Sergio Ramirez, Dora Maria Téllez, Victor Tirado Lopez, Henry Ruiz, Luis Carrion, Victor Hugo Tinoco and Monica Baltodano.

In 1996, Arnoldo Aleman, a liberal candidate, supported by UNO organizations, won the presidential elections against Daniel Ortega. This appeared to be a victory for the former Contras, most of whom were of liberal tradition, while Colonel Bermudez's widow campaigned for Aleman.[25] It was only after this election that the *Recontras* gradually laid down their arms. While the presidency of this former Somoza supporter was marked by numerous corruption and money laundering scandals, Ortega did not hesitate to reach an agreement with him to share power management positions. Despite this, in 2001, Ortega was defeated a third time in the presidential elections against the liberal Enrique Bolaños.

It was with a moderate or even conservative program on the issue of abortion, but still revolutionary rhetoric, that Ortega ran again in the 2006 elections that he finally won. He took the lead in a country that remained one of the poorest in Latin America and quickly

Together with Angola and Afghanistan, the war in Nicaragua of the 1980s is widely considered the third major 'hot' battlefield of the Cold War. It was also the only one in which the Soviet-supported side won a clear-cut military victory. This was possible only because the FSLN never spoiled its relations with the majority of the Nicaraguan population, and thus remained capable of running a continuous military build-up – like these irregulars of one of the BLIs. (Albert Grandolini Collection)

showed authoritarian tendencies and repressed dissenting voices. On the military level, Ortega's return to power led once again to a politicisation of the army. In 2014, he increased presidential power over the military and appointed many Sandinistas to important positions. Also under pressure, the EN grew closer to Russia, which in 2016 supplied 20 T-72B1 tanks to Nicaragua.[26] Ortega was also getting closer to Chavez's Venezuela and his country joined the Bolivarian Alliance for the Americas in 2007.

In October 2009, Ortega succeeded in having the constitutional law abolished which prohibited a president from being re-elected, allowing him to win a new term in 2011. Five years later, in 2016, he won the presidential elections again with his wife, Rosario Murillo, as vice-president. This new mandate was marked by a major political crisis that erupted on 18 April 2018 with the launch of a movement to challenge the government in place, following the announcement of a social security reform project. Demonstrations and roadblocks were regularly organized until July. In June, Ortega's opponents built barricades in Masaya. The repression by the police and the shock troops of the FSLN, the turbas, was violent and the human toll of this protest was heavy: nearly 325 dead and more than 2,000 wounded.[27] A national dialogue commission was created on 17 May, under the mediation of the Church, to work towards an end to the crisis, but its work remained suspended. On 10 January 2019, Rafael Solis, a Supreme Court judge close to Ortega, resigned from his position and the FSLN to denounce repression and the lack of democracy. At the time of writing a political crisis scenario similar to that in Venezuela cannot be ruled out. The lava is still smouldering under the Nicaraguan volcano.

The end of the Nicaraguan conflict in 1990 was one of those paradoxes with which history is filled. Indeed, as a decade of armed conflict came to an end, the Sandinistas who dominated their opponents militarily were nevertheless driven out of power.

The EPS had demonstrated a tactical mobility far superior to the Contras, based on modern equipment adapted to the counter-insurgency war, but also on soldiers, mostly urban conscripts educated and motivated by a revolutionary nationalism associated a strong anti-Americanism whose morale was high. The Sandinista counter-insurgency strategy had been particularly effective in preventing the Contras from operating in the densely populated and urbanized areas of the Pacific region. The latter never managed to establish a liberated area in the country and remained confined to the vast sparsely populated areas of the north and east, where they faced increasing logistical difficulties.

Strategically defeated, the Contras would have collapsed without US support. Their weaknesses were numerous. They were divided and each faction favoured different goals. Even when, from 1985, a unification movement took place, they failed to define a political program beyond a few simple objectives such as the defeat of the Sandinistas and free elections. There were also differences between the motives of ordinary combatants, commanders and Miami politicians as evidenced by the crisis that erupted after the signing of the Sapoá Accords. The greatest weakness of the Contras, however, was their dependence on the United States and the political compromises that were made in Washington. Indeed, in order not to upset Congress, the Reagan Administration had to limit its involvement in the Nicaraguan conflict and the help it provided to the Contras, if it allowed them to continue fighting, remained insufficient to win. They also failed to gain broad support in the population. Although their location was important in the northern, central and Atlantic regions of the country, these were the least populated and least rich areas of Nicaragua. They found no support in the cities as the FSLN had done before 1979 and which allowed them to overthrow Somoza.

The only major success of the Contras, and also thus of the Reagan administration, was to force the Sandinista government to mobilize more and more economic resources to deal with them. This was where the Sandinista defeat in 1990 was played out. The FSLN continued to increase military spending while the economic situation continued to deteriorate. At the end of the decade, the system was out of breath and the population, tired of war and shortages, aspired to a better life and change, an aspiration of which the Sandinistas were the victims in the polls.

Only Washington's assistance to the Contras allowed them to continue a war they could not win. The United States had given approximately $320 million to the Contras.[28] In addition to this amount, $55 million was provided in 1985 and 1986 by Saudi Arabia, Taiwan, Brunei, US billionaires or by the embezzlement of funds in the Irangate case. For its part, the Soviet Union provided economic assistance of $300 to $400 million and $650 to $700 million was provided by the GDR, Bulgaria, Cuba and Libya. Without the support provided to each side by the two superpowers, the civil war would not have had the scale and duration it had. Although, it ended when Moscow and Washington came together to end the Cold War.

While Nicaragua remained a relatively secondary front of the Cold War, the toll of the conflict was heavy for this small country of only three million people. During the war, 30,000 men fought for the Contras and about 300,000 in the EPS.[29] From 1980 to 1989, the war caused the deaths of 61,826 people, 60% of whom died between 1986 and 1989 and nearly 700,000 people were displaced.[30] There were many abuses against civilians by both sides. In 1986, an Amnesty International report to the US Congress denounced the "torture and murder" committed by the Contras and the extrajudicial executions carried out by Sandinista troops. That same year, the Washington Office on Latin America recorded 139 cases of abuse, 21 of which were committed by Sandinistas.[31] In addition to the human losses and violence, the economy was in ruins. At the end of the war, Nicaragua once again became one of the poorest countries in Latin America. Nevertheless, since 1990, Nicaragua had been learning about democracy, in a long and difficult process as shown by the events of 2018.

Selected Bibliography

Anderson, Michael John, *Puppet Wars: The Nicaraguan Revolution in a Cold War Context* (Western Oregon University, 2003).

Aguilera, Gabriel, *El Fusil y el Olivo: la cuestion militar en Centroamerica* (Flacso, 1989).

Aravena, Francisco, 'La Unión Soviética y Centroamérica', *Foro Internacional*, vol. 28, n°4, April-June 1988.

Avilés Farré, Juan, 'Dos guerras en Nicaragua, 1978-1988', *Espacio, Tiempo y Forma*, t. 4, 1991.

Barbosa Miranda, Francisco, *Síntesis de la historia militar de Nicaragua* (Centro de Historia militar-ejercito de Nicaragua, 2007).

Bataillon, Gilles, 'et Recontras nicaraguayens (1982-1993): réflexions sur l'action armée et la constitution d'acteurs politico-militaires', *Cultures & Conflits*, vol. 12, n°4, 1993.

Bataillon, Gilles, 'Comandantes, état-major et guérilleros: jeux de pouvoirs à l'intérieur de la guérilla miskitu (Nicaragua, 1981-1984)', *Cahiers des Amériques latines*, 36, 2001.

Bataillon, Gilles, *Genèse des guerres internes en Amérique centrale (1960-1983)*, Les Belles Lettres, 2003.

Bataillon, Gilles, 'De Sandino aux Contras. Formes et pratique de la guerre au Nicaragua', *Annales HSS*, n°3, -may-june 2005.

Benitez, Raul (ed), *EE. UU contra Nicaragua. La guerra de baja intensidad en Centroamérica* (Editorial Revolucion, 1987).

Bernd, Georges E., *Border jumping: Strategic and Operational considerations in planning cross-border raids against insurgent sanctuaries*, (Naval Postgraduate School, 2013).

Blank, Stephen, 'Soviet Foreign Policy and Conflict Resolution in the Third World: The Nicaraguan Civil War', *Conflict Quaterly*, Fall 1993.

Bulmer Thomas, Victor, 'Nicaragua desde 1930' in Leslie Bethell (ed), *Historia de America latina, 14. America Central desde 1930*, Critica, 2001.

Burke, Kyle, *Revolutionaries for the Right. Anticommunist Internationalism and Paramilitary Warfare in the Cold War* (University of North Carolina Press, 2018).

Burton-Vulovic, Nicholas, *Contra-Directory: Threat Perception and US Policy toward Nicaragua (1979-1990)* (University of Victoria, 2013).

Brown, Timothy Charles, *When the AK-47s Fall Silent. Revolutionaries, Guerrillas and the dangers of Peace* (Hoover Institution Press, 2000).

Cassel, Sarah, *A Proxy War or A Struggle for National Liberation: The Ideological Motivations and Human Rights Considerations of the United States-Contra Alliance* (Wesleyan University Managua, 2012).

Brown, Timothy Charles, *The Real Contra War: Highlander Peasant Resistance in Nicaragua* (University of Oklahoma Press, 2001).

Castillo Rivas, Donald, *Gringos, contras y sandinistas: Testimonio de una guerra civil en Nicaragua* (TM Editores, 1993).

Comandancia General del Ejército de Nicaragua, *Ejército de Nicaragua, 30 años de vida instiucional: (1979-2009)* (Ejército de Nicaragua, 2009).

Coste, Françoise, *Reagan* (Tempus, 2018).

Del Pino, Rafael, *Inside Castro's Bunker* (CreateSpace, 2012).

Dominguez Reyes, Edme, 'La politica sovietica y cubana hacia Nicaragua: 1979-1989', *Papers, Revista de Sociologia*, 1990.

Draghir, Wassim, 'American Foreign Policy Fiascos: US Policy in Nicaragua as a Case Study', *Advances in Social Science Research Journal*, Vol. 4, N° 8, April 2017.

Ferrero Blanco, María-Dolores, 'Daniel Ortega y Mijail Gorbachov. Nicaragua y la URSS en los ultimos anos de la guerra fria', *Hispania Nova. Revista de Historia contemporanea*, n° 13, 2015.

Gleieses, Piero, *Visions of Freedom, Havana, Washington, Pretoria, and the Struggle for Southern Africa, 1976-1991* (The University of North Carolina Press, 2013).

Harto de Vera, Fernando, 'La URSS y la revolución sandinista: los estrechos límites de la solidaridad soviética', *Africa-America Latina. Cuadernos*, n°7, 1992.

Hernandez Ruigomez, Manuel, *La Nicaragua sandinista y las elecciones de febrero 1990: transición a la democracia o alternancia democratica* (Universidas Complutense de Madrid, 2012).

Hernandez Sanchez-Barba, Mario, 'Nicaragua y el Ejército sandinista', *Cuadernos de Estrategia*, n°48, 1992.

Horton, Lynn, *Peasants in Arms: War and Peace in the Mountains of Nicaragua, 1979-1994* (Ohio University Press, 1999).

Kagan, Robert, *A Twilight Struggle: American Power and Nicaragua, 1977-1990* (The Free Press, 1996).

Keen, Benjamin and Haynes, Keith, *A History of Latin America* (Houghton Mifflin Company, 2000).

Kinzer, Stephen, *Blood and Brothers. Life and War in Nicaragua* (Putnam, 1991).

Krujit, Dirk, 'Revolucion y contrarevolucion: el gobierno sandinista y la guerra de la Contra en Nicaragua, 1980-1990', *Desafios*, 23-II, 2011.

Krujit, Dirk, *Guerrillas: War and Peace in Central America* (Zed Books, 2008).

Martí i Puig, Salvador, *La Révolución enredada, Nicaragua, 1977-1996*, Los Libros de la Catarata, 1997.

Martí i Puig, Salvador, *The Origins of the Peasant-Contra Rebellion in Nicaragua, 1979-87* (Institute of Latin American Studies, University of London, 2001).

McCarl, James, *Sandinista Counterinsurgency Tactics* (Fort Leavenworth, 1990).

Moreno, Luis, *Principio y fin de la guerra de los contras* (CreateSpace, 2016).

Pérez, Justiniano, *El Ejército de los Somozas: auge, caida y secuela de su extincion* (Editora de Arte, 2010).

Pestana Randy and Latell, Brian, *Nicaraguan Military Culture* (Florida International University, 2017).

Pozas Pardo, Santiago, *Nicaragua (1979-1989), Actor singular de las relaciones internacionales en el final de la Guerra fría* (Universidad del Pais Vasco, 2000).

Prevost, Gary, 'The "Contra" War in Nicaragua', *Conflict Quaterly*, Summer 1987.

Richmond, John D., *The Armed Citizen Pillar of Democracy* (Air Command and Staff College Air University, 2010).

Robinson, William I and Norsworthy, Kent, *David and Goliath. The US war against Nicaragua* (Monthly Review Press, 1987).

Spencer, David E., 'El Comando de Fuerzas Especiales (COE) de Nicaragua: Como combinar las mejores tacticas, técnicas y procedimientos de Oriente y Occidente', *Military Review*, July-August 2013.

Storkmann, Klaus, 'East German Military Aid to the Sandinista Government of Nicaragua (1979-1990)', *Journal of Cold War Studies*, Vol 16, n°2, Spring 2016.

Thaler, Kai M., *From Insurgents to Incumbents: Revolutionary State Building in Nicaragua* (Harvard University, 2015).

Travis, Philip, *Outlaw States: The United-States, Nicaragua and the Cold War root of the War on Terror* (Washington State University, 2014).

Vickers, Robert, 'Intelligence and Punta Huete Airfield: A Symbol of Past Soviet/Russian Strategic Interest in Central America', Studies in Intelligence, Vol 60, n°2, june 2016.

Walker, Thomas W., *Nicaragua, Living in the Shadow of the Eagle* (Westview Press, 2003).

Weathers, Bynum E, *Guerilla Warfare in Nicaragua* (Air University Research Study, 1983).

Wyatt Medina, Benjamin, *The Myth of Unity: The Contra War, 1980-1989* (College of William and Mary, 2016).

Wilson, Andrew W., *Conflict beyond Borders: The International Dimensions of Nicaragua's Violent Twentieth-Century, 1909-1990* (University of Nebraska, 2016).

Zaremba, Lauren M., *Nicaragua: Before and After the Revolution* (Southern Illinois University, 1992).

Further information used in this book was obtained on diverse websites and online archives such as those of the cia.org, nsa.org, the Library of Congress Country Studies, biblioteca.ccoo.cat (Biblioteca de l'Arxiu Historic de CCOO de Catalunya), uacm.edu.mx (Universitad Autonoma de Mexico).

Notes

Chapter 1

1. Dirk Krujit, 'Revolucion y contrarevolucion: el gobierno sandinista y la guerra de la Contra en Nicaragua, 1980-1990', *Desafios*, 23-II, 2011 (henceforth Krujit), p. 56.
2. Juan Avilés Farré, 'Dos Guerras en Nicaragua: 1978-1988', *Espacio, Tiempo y Forma*, 1991, p. 302.
3. Krujit, p. 57.
4. Juan Avilés Farré, p. 303.
5. Alain Rouquié, *Les forces politiques en Amérique centrale*, Karthala,1991, p. 197.
6. Ibid, p. 196.
7. Laura M. Zaremba, *Nicaragua: Before and After the Revolution*, Southern Illinois University, 1992, p. 38.
8. Ibid, p. 38.
9. Krujit, p. 63.
10. Salvador Martí y Puig, *The Origins of the Peasant-Contra Rebellion in Nicaragua, 1979-87* (Institute of Latin American Studies, University of London, 2001), p. 6.
11. Gary Prevost, 'The"Contra"War in Nicaragua ', *Conflict Quaterly*, Summer 1987, p. 5.
12. Edme Dominguez Reyes, 'La politica sovietica y cubana hacia Nicaragua: 1979-1989', *Papers, Revista de Sociologia*, 1990, p. 108.
13. Fernando Harto de Vera, 'La URSS y la revolución sandinista: los estrechos límites de la solidaridad soviética', *Africa-America Latina. Cuadernos*, n°7, 1992, p. 88.
14. Ibid, p. 89.
15. Laura M. Zaremba, p. 40. Dolores Ferrero Blanco, 'Daniel Ortega y Mijail Gorbachov. Nicaragua y la URSS en los ultimos anos de la guerra fria', *Hispania Nova. Revista de Historia contemporanea*, n° 13, 2015, p. 31.

Chapter 2

1. Dirk Kruijt, *Guerrillas: War and Peace in Central America* (Zed Books, 2008), p. 35.
2. Mario Hernandez Sanchez-Barba, 'Nicaragua y el Ejército sandinista', *Cuadernos de Estrategia*, n°48, 1992, p. 59.
3. Lacayo retained this position until 1995. In February 1980 he also became Deputy Minister of Defence.
4. Krujit, p. 62. Bernardino Larios was a lieutenant colonel before being fired in 1978 after being accused of plotting against Somoza. Some time after his removal from his position as Minister of War, he was imprisoned. He was finally released in March 1984 and exiled to Costa Rica a year later.
5. Comandancia General del Ejército de Nicaragua, *Ejército de Nicaragua, 30 años de vida institucional: (1979-2009)*, Ejército de Nicaragua, 2009, p. 51.
6. Ibid, p. 53-54.
7. Ibid, p. 55.
8. Piero Gleieses, *Visions of Freedom, Havana, Washington, Pretoria, and the Struggle for Southern Africa, 1976-1991* (The University of North Carolina Press, 2013), p. 320.
9. *Newsweek*, 19 november 1984.
10. *NYT*, 7 June 1985.
11. Rafael del Pino, *Inside Castro's Bunker*, (CreateSpace, 2012), p. 190-191. Rafal del Pino was a high-ranking Cuban air force officer, and defected to the United States in the late 1980s. Since then, he has been a fierce opponent of the Cuban regime.
12. Comandancia General del Ejército de Nicaragua, p. 98.
13. Troops of border guards were commanded by Commandante Francisco Rivera.
14. Mario Hernandez Sanchez-Barba, p. 60.
15. Comandancia General del Ejército de Nicaragua, p. 100.
16. *NYT*, 10 April 1983.
17. Laura M. Zaremba, p. 32.
18. Krujit, p. 72.
19. *NYT*, 2 January 1985.
20. *NYT*, 12 September 1986.
21. Salvador Martí y Puig, p. 29.
22. *The Sandinista Military Build-up*, US Department of Defence, 1987, p. 3.
23. Krujit, p. 73.
24. Rafael del Pino, p. 191. *New York Times* (henceforth *NYT*), 19 June 1983.
25. Robert Vickers, 'Intelligence and Punta Huete Airfield: A Symbol of Past Soviet/Russian Strategic Interest in Central America', Studies in Intelligence, Vol 60, n°2, june 2016, p. 14.
26. Fernando Harto de Vera, p. 92. From 1985, by decision of the Managua government, the number of Cuban military advisers continued to decrease.
27. Piero Gleieses, p. 320.
28. http://www.chekist.ru/article/3896
29. Klaus Storkmann, 'East German Military Aid to the Sandinista Government of Nicaragua (1979-1990)', *Journal of Cold War Studies*, Vol 16, n°2, Spring 2016, p. 59.
30. Ibid, p. 63.
31. Nicholas Burton-Vulovic, *Contra-Directory: Threat Perception and US Policy toward Nicaragua (1979-1990)* (University of Victoria, 2013), p. 43.
32. Robert Vickers, p. 14.
33. Stephan Blank, 'Soviet Foreign Policy and Conflict Resolution in the Third World: The Nicaraguan Civil War', *Conflict Quaterly*, Fall 1993, p. 9.
34. Comandancia General del Ejército de Nicaragua, p. 105.
35. *The Sandinista Military Build-up*, p. 5.
36. Gabriel Aguilera, *El Fusil y el Olivo: la cuestion militar en Centroamerica*, Flacso, 1989, p. 157.
37. *The Sandinista Military Build-up*, US Department of Defence, 1985, p. 11.
38. *The Sandinista Military Build-up*, 1987, p. 6.
39. Comandancia General del Ejército de Nicaragua, p. 118.
40. *The Sandinista Military Build-up*, 1985, p. 29.
41. Comandancia General del Ejército de Nicaragua, p. 120.
42. Rafael del Pino, p. 184.
43. Ibid, p. 185.
44. Ibid, p. 185-190.
45. Robert Vickers, p. 15.
46. *NYT*, 27 October 1985.
47. *NYT*, 10 July 1986. Notably, diverse reports about higher or lower numbers of Soviet-made helicopters delivered to Nicaragua cannot be confirmed (for example: 12 Mi-8Ts and 48 Mi-17s). On the contrary, although these were issued in sequence, they still contained significant gaps: nevertheless,

48 *NYT*, 7 April 1987.
49 Comandancia General del Ejército de Nicaragua, pp. 112-113.
50 Rafael del Pino, p. 185.
51 Robert Vickers, p. 18.
52 *The Sandinista Military Build-up*, 1987, p. 10.
53 Gabriel Aguilera, p. 157-158; Flintham, pp. 361-365.
54 Kai M. Thaler, *From Insurgents to Incumbents: Revolutionary State Building in Nicaragua* (Harvard University, 2015), p. 28.
55 David E. Spencer, 'El Comando de Fuerzas Especiales (COE) de Nicaragua: Como combinar las mejores tacticas, técnicas y proceimientos de Oriente y Occidente', *Military Review*, July-August 2013, p. 70.
56 Alain Rouquié, p. 202.

Chapter 3

1 Krujit, p. 67.
2 Alain Rouquié, p. 207.
3 Krujit, p. 66.
4 Alain Rouquié, p. 221-222.
5 Ibid, p. 204.
6 Stephen Kinzer, *Blood of Brothers, Life and War in Nicaragua* (Harvard University, 2007), pp. 83-84.
7 Francisco Barbosa Miranda, *Sintesis de la historia militar de Nicaragua* (Centro de Historia-militar erjército de Nicaragua, 2007), p. 58.
8 Stephen Kinzer, p. 138.
9 Krujit, p. 70.
10 Kyle Burke, *Revolutionaries for the Right. Anticommunist Internationalism and Paramilitary Warfare in the Cold War* (University of North Carolina Press, 2018), p. 136.
11 Justiniano Pérez, *El Ejército de los Somozas: auge, caida y secuela de su extincion* (Editora de Arte, 2010), pp. 81-84.
12 Thimothy Charles Brown, *The Real Contra War: Highlander Peasant Resistance in Nicaragua* (University of Oklahoma Press, 2001), pp. 84-85.
13 Luis Moreno, *Principio y fin de la guerra de los contras* (CreateSpace, 2016), p. 13.
14 Timothy C. Brown, pp. 74-76.
15 *El Pais*, 9 June 1985. Stephen Kinzer, p. 141.
16 Kyle Burke, p. 137.
17 Timoty C. Brown, p. 87.
18 Donald Castillo Rivas, *Gringos, contras y sandinistas: Testimonio de una guerra civil en Nicaragua* (TM Editores, 1993), p. 89.
19 Krujit, p. 68.
20 Gilles Bataillon, 'et reContras nicaraguayens (1982-1993): réflexions sur l'action armée et la constitution d'acteurs politico-militaires', *Cultures & Conflits*, vol. 12, n°4, 1993, p. 67.
21 Timothy C. Brown, *When the AK-47s Fall Silent. Revolutionaries, Guerilla and the dangers of Peace* (Hoover Institution Press, 2000), pp. 212-213.
22 Kinzer, p. 260.
23 *El Pais*, 4 October 1980.
24 After being banned, the MISURASATA became the MISURATA (Miskito, Suma, Rama United).
25 About 10,000 Miskitos found refuge in Honduras, Stephen Kinzer, p. 262.
26 Justiniano Pérez, p. 91.
27 Donald Castillo Rivas, p. 90.
28 Ibid, p. 91.
29 Lynn Horton, *Peasants in Arms: War and Peace in the Mountains of Nicaragua, 1979-1994* (Ohio University Press, 1999), p. 104.
30 Ibid, p. 109.
31 Timothy C. Brown, *The Real Contra War*, p. 14.
32 Timothy C. Brown, *When the AK-47s Fall Silent*, pp. 143-147.
33 Lynn Horton, p. 112-113.
34 Ibid, p. 114.
35 Ibid, p. 96.
36 Timothy C. Brown, *When the AK-47s Fall Silent*, pp. 147-148.
37 Lynn Horton, p. 116.
38 Timothy C. Brown, *The Real Contra War*, p. 87.
39 Gilles Bataillon, p. 69.
40 Lynn Horton 1979-1994, p. 118.
41 Timothy C. Brown, *When the AK-47s Fall Silent*, pp. 172.
42 Timothy C. Brown, *The Real Contra War*, p. 88.
43 Ibid, p. 87.
44 Luis Moreno, p. 19. Timothy C. Brown, *When the AK-47s Fall Silent*, p. 163.
45 Luis Moreno, p. 20.
46 Timothy C. Brown, *The Real Contra War*, pp. 98-99.
47 Comarca was a traditional local administrative division.
48 Timothy C. Brown, *The Real Contra War*, p. 95.
49 Francisco Barbosa Miranda, p. 59.
50 Luis Moreno, p. 122.
51 Francisco Barbosa Miranda, p. 59.
52 Timothy C. Brown, *The Real Contra War*, pp. 106-107 .
53 The FDN ideology was set out in a document known as the 'Blue and White Book', p. 138.

Chapter 4

1 Françoise Coste, *Reagan*, Tempus, 2018, p. 499.
2 Stephen Kinzer, p. 97.
3 Nicaragua: *The Price of Intervention. Reagan's War against the Sandinistas* (Institute for Policy Studies, 1987) p. 327.
4 Laura M. Zaremba, p. 40.
5 Gary Prevost, p. 5.
6 Ibid, p. 6.
7 *Barricada internacional*, 4 October 1982.
8 Gary Prevost, p. 7.
9 *Barricada internacional*, 1 August 1983.
10 Covert Action Information Bulletin, n°22, Fall 1984, p. 26.
11 http://www.country-data.com/cgi-bin/query/r-5731.html
12 *Barricada internacional*, 9 May 1983.
13 Philip Travis, *Outlaw States: The United-States, Nicaragua and the Cold War root of the War on Terror* (Washington State University, 2014), p. 33.
14 Françoise Coste, p. 501.
15 *NYT*, 13 June 1983.
16 Stephen Kinzer, pp. 99.
17 *Newsweek*, 25 August 1986, p. 37.
18 *Barricada internacional*, 16 May 1983.
19 Stephen Kinzer, p. 291.
20 Françoise Coste, p. 501-502.
21 Stephen Kinzer, p. 97.
22 Françoise Coste, p. 503.
23 The UDN-FARN broke with the FDN at the beginning of 1982 and left Honduras to settle in Costa Rica.
24 Krujit, p. 71.
25 *El Pais*, 18 April 1984. Sarah Cassel, *A Proxy War or A Struggle for National Liberation: The Ideological Motivations and Human Rights Considerations of the United States-Contra Alliance* (Wesleyan University Managua, 2012), p. 18.
26 Gilles Bataillon, p. 2-3.
27 *El Pais*, 25 June 1983.
28 *El Pais*, 17 July 1982.
29 Thimothy C. Brown, *When the AK-47s Fall Silent*, p. 216.
30 *Barricada internacional*, 18 October 1982.
31 Stephen Kinzer, p. 146.
32 *El Pais*, 9 June 1985.
33 Luis Moreno, p. 19.
34 Ibid, pp. 24-42.
35 *El Pais*, 24 July 1982.
36 *Barricada internacional*, 4 Octobrer 1982.
37 *Barricada internacional*, 14 February 1983.
38 Luis Moreno, pp 17.
39 Ibid, p. 151.
40 Ibid, p. 176.
41 Ibid, p. 42.
42 *El Pais*, 20 January 1983.
43 Alain Rouquié, p. 205.
44 Ibid, p. 151 & 'Thirty Seconds over Managua', *Time*, 19 September 1983.
45 Ibid, p. 176 & Chuck deCaro, 'American Mercs Tough it Out', *Gung-Ho*, June 1988.
46 'Flying the Unfriendly Skies', *Time*, 30 April 1984.
47 Flintham, p. 265.

Chapter 5
1. *El Pais*, 20 March 1983.
2. *Barricada internacional*, 20 December 1982.
3. Luis Moreno, pp. 57-58.
4. *Barricada internacional*, 28 March 1983.
5. Comandancia General del Ejército de Nicaragua, p. 62.
6. Thimothy C. Brown, *When the AK-47s Fall Silent*, p. 175.
7. Luis Moreno, p. 65.
8. *Ibid*, pp. 67-68.
9. *El Pais*, 20 Marc 1983.
10. *Barricada internacional*, 11 April 1983.
11. *Barricada internacional*, 25 April 1983.
12. *Barricada internacional*, 2 and 9 May 1983.
13. *Barricada internacional*, 16 May 1983.
14. *Barricada internacional*, 30 May 1983.
15. *NYT*, 19 June 1983.
16. *Barricada internacional*, 11 July and 1 August 1983.
17. *Barricada internacional*, 22 August 1983.
18. *Barricada internacional*, 5 September 1983.
19. *Barricada internacional*, 13 May 1983.
20. *El Pais*, 31 May 1983.
21. *Barricada internacional*, 11 July and 8 August 1983.
22. *Barricada internacional*, 19 September 1983.
23. William I. Robinson, Kent Norsworthy, *David and Goliath. The US War Against Nicaragua*, Monthly Review Press, 1987, p. 71.
24. Luis Moreno, p. 70.
25. *Barricada internacional*, 15 August 1983.
26. 'Thirty Seconds over Managua', *Time*, 19 September 1983.
27. *Barricada internacional*, 19 September 1983.
28. *El Pais*, 25 September 1983.
29. *Covert Action Information Bulletin*, n°20, Winter 1984, p. 29.
30. *Barricada internacional*, 10 October 1983.
31. *Barricada internacional*, 17 October 1983.
32. Luis Moreno, p. 91.
33. *Ibid*, p. 98-99.
34. *Ibid* p. 108.
35. NYT, 26 *September* 1983.
36. Luis Moreno, p. 140.
37. *Ibid*, p. 17.
38. Lynn Horton, p. 126.
39. Salvador Martí y Puig, p. 31.
40. Luis Moreno, p. 75.
41. *Barricada internacional*, 9 May 1983.
42. *Barricada internacional*, 29 August 1983.
43. *NYT*, 26 August 1983.
44. *El Pais*, 30 September 1983, *Barricada internacional*, 10 October 1983.
45. Luis Moreno, p. 77-83.
46. *NYT*, 9 December 1983.
47. Luis Moreno, p. 116.
48. *Ibid*, p. 125-126.
49. *El Pais*, 17 April 1984.
50. *NYT*, 21 April 1984.
51. *NYT*, 16 June 1984.
52. Kinzer, p. 235.
53. *NYT*, 12 April 1984.
54. *NYT*, 29 August 1984.
55. *Covert Action Information Bulletin*, n°22, Fall 1984, p. 27.
56. *NYT*, 23 November 1984.
57. *NYT*, 3 March 1984.
58. *NYT*, 16 January 1984.
59. The mining of ports was carried out by a CIA task force called *Unilaterally Controlled Latino Assets*, which included only Hispanic foreign-born agents, Stephen Kinzer, p. 229.
60. Nicholas Burton-Vulovic, p. 71.
61. *NYT*, 12 April 1984.
62. Gary Prevost, p. 13.
63. Stephen Kinzer, pp. 232-235.
64. Alain Rouquié, p. 235.
65. Donald Castillo Rivas, p. 92.
66. *Covert Action Information Bulletin*, n°18, Winter 1983, p. 32.
67. **Gilles Bataillon**, '*Comandantes*, état-major et guérilleros: jeux de pouvoirs à l'intérieur de la guérilla miskitu (Nicaragua, 1981-1984)', *Cahiers des Amériques latines*, 36 | 2001, pp. 127-160.
68. Justiniano Pérez, p. 95.
69. Stephen Kinzer, p. 263.
70. Donald Castillo Rivas, p. 93.
71. Kinzer, p. 268.
72. *NYT*, 12 April 1984.
73. Françoise Coste, p. 504.
74. *NYT*, 16 January 1984.

Chapter 6
1. *NYT*, 15 March 1983.
2. Lynn Horton, p. 122.
3. *NYT*, 10 April 1983.
4. *Barricada internacional*, 11 October 1982 and 7 March 1983.
5. Thimothy C. Brown, *The Real Contra War*, p. 65.
6. Lynn Horton, p. 128.
7. *NYT*, 16 June 1984.
8. Krujit, p. 71-72.
9. Christopher Paul, Colin P. Clark, Beth Grill, 'Fathers. Detailed Counterinsurgency Case Studies' (Rand Corporation, 2010), p. 70.
10. *NYT*, 26 Decembrer 1986.
11. *Barricada internacional*, 25 April 1983.
12. *Barricada internacional*, 20 November 1986.
13. *Barricada internacional*, 22 November 1982.
14. *El Pais*, 23 May 1983.
15. *El Pais*, 27 March 1985.
16. *Barricada internacional*, 14 February 1983. *NYT*, 16 June 1984.
17. Luis Moreno, p. 122.
18. Ibid, p. 124-125.
19. *El Pais*, 9 June 1985.
20. James Mccarl, *Sandinista Counterinsurgency Tactics*, Fort Leavenworth,, 1990, p. 57.
21. *El Pais*, 15 July 1983.
22. *Barricada internacional*, 30 May 1983.
23. *Barricada internacional*, 7 August 1986.
24. *The Nicaraguan Resistance and US Policy. Report on a May 1987 Conference*, Rand Corporation, June 1989, p. 38.
25. David E. Spencer, p. 71.
26. Comandancia General del Ejército de Nicaragua, p. 103.
27. Luis Moreno, p. 158.
28. James Mccarl, p. 43.
29. Ibid, pp. 84-85.
30. Ibid, p. 51.
31. *NYT*, 9 September 1985.
32. *NYT*, 17 April 1983.
33. *NYT*, 3 January 1985.
34. *Barricada internacional*, 24 July 1986.
35. *NYT*, 23 *January* 1985.
36. Luis Moreno, p. 168-171.
37. *El Pais*, 11 May 1985.
38. *NYT*, 2 September 1985.
39. *Barricada internactional*, 14 August 1986.
40. Luis Moreno, p. 173.
41. Ibid, pp. 172-173.
42. *El Pais*, 18 May 1985.
43. *El Pais*, 10 June 1985.
44. Justiniano Pérez, p. 97.
45. Gilles Bataillon, 'Contras et reContras nicaraguayens (1982-1993)', p. 14.
46. *NYT*, 4 June 1985.
47. Luis Moreno, p. 165.
48. Ibid, p. 165-166.
49. *El Pais*, 13 May 1985.
50. *NYT*, 4 June 1985.
51. Luis Moreno, p. 166-167.

48. John Piowaty, 'Contra Air: Secord's Central American Flying Circus', *Soldier of Fortune*, October 1987.
49. Ibid, p. 42.

52 Ibid, p. 175-177.
53 *NYT*, 30 March 1986.
54 *El Pais*, 27 March 1986.
55 *Boletin informativo Honduras*, April 1986.
56 Philip Travis, *Outlaw States: The United-States, Nicaragua and the Cold War Root of the War on Terror* (Washington State University, 2014), p. 200.
57 Luis Moreno, p. 176-177.
58 Ibid, p. 182-191.
59 Ibid, p. 163.
60 Stephen Kinzer, p. 270.
61 *NYT*, 29 July 1985.
62 Donald Castillo Rivas, p. 93.
63 Gary Prevost, p. 13.
64 Donald Castillo Rivas, p. 95.
65 Alain Rouquié, p. 198-199.

Chapter 7

1 Stephen Kinzer, p. 292-293.
2 Françoise Coste, p. 506.
3 John K. Singlaub, born in 1921, was OSS officer during the Second World War. He headed CIA operations in Manchuria during the Chinese Civil War, led American troops in the Korean War and managed the secret war in Laos and Vietnam. In 1977, he criticised Carter's policy and was relieved from his position in Korea. Singlaub was founder, in 1981, of the United States Council for World Freedom, the US chapter of the World Anti-Communist League (WACL).
4 Kyle Burke, p. 142.
5 Ibid, p. 145.
6 *Soldier of Fortune*, October 1987, p. 34.
7 Kyle Burke, p. 147.
8 Walter Bruyère-Ostells, *Les volontaires armés*, Nouveau Monde, 2018.
9 *NYT*, 8 July 1985.
10 *NYT*, 11 November 1985.
11 Françoise Coste, p. 577-578.
12 Ibid, p. 605.
13 Ibid, p. 621.
14 Luis Moreno, p. 164.
15 Stephen Kinzer, p. 310.
16 Ibid, p. 311.
17 Kyle Burke, p. 152-153.
18 https://nsarchive2.gwu.edu//NSAEBB/NSAEBB113/north06.pdf
19 *Barricada internacional*, 20 November 1986.
20 *Time*, 20 October 1986.
21 Stephen Kinzer, p. 313.
22 Luis Moreno, p. 160.
23 Stephen Kinzer, pp. 300-301.
24 Wassim Draghir, 'American Foreign Policy Fiascos: US Policy in Nicaragua as a Case Study', *Advances in Social Science Research Journal*, Vol. 4, N° 8, April 2017, p. 93.
25 *El Pais*, 27 July 1984.
26 William I. Robinson, Kent Norsworthy, p. 236.
27 *El Pais*, 1 February 1987.
28 Gary Prevost, p. 12.
29 *El Pais*, 8 May 1987.
30 Donald Castillo Rivas, p. 92-93.
31 *El Pais*, 26 December 1986.
32 *El Pais*, 25 November 1986.
33 The FDN received 178 Redeye missiles.
34 Stephen Kinzer, p. 341 & Luis Moreno, p. 180-181.
35 Ibid, p. 306.
36 Philip Travis, p. 163.
37 James Mccarl, p. 86.
38 Comandancia General del Ejército de Nicaragua, p. 67.
39 Luis Moreno, p. 191-192.
40 *NYT*, 23 May 1987.
41 Luis Moreno, p. 194.
42 *NYT*, 10 June 1987.
43 Luis Moreno, p. 193.
44 John Cushman Jr., 'The Stinger Missile: Helping to Change the Course of a War', *The New York Times*, 17 January 1988.
45 Stephen Kinzer, p. 344.
46 Gary Prevost, p. 13.
47 The Contadora group sponsored by Panama, Colombia, Venezuela and Mexico wanted to maintain the stability and security of Central America by seeking an agreement between Washington and Managua.
48 *Barricada*, 11 October 1987.
49 *NYT*, 11 August 1986.
50 Stephen Kinzer, pp. 347-348.
51 Ibid, p. 350.
52 Edme Dominguez Reyes, p. 106.
53 Wassim Draghir, p. 87.
54 *El Pais*, 8 October 1987.
55 Ibid.
56 RAAS: Región Autónoma del Atlántico Sur (South Atlantic Autonomous Region).
57 Luis Moreno, p. 195.
58 Ibid, p. 195-196.
59 *El Pais*, 24 December 1987 and Thimothy C. Brown, *The Real Contra War*, p. 105-106.
60 *Time*, 4 January 1988.
61 *El Pais*, 22 December 1987.
62 Luis Moreno, p. 198.
63 Donald Castillo Rivas, p. 98-106 and Alain Rouquié, p. 236.
64 Stephen Kinzer, pp. 364-365.
65 Comandancia General del Ejército de Nicaragua, pp. 72-73.
66 Robert Kagan, *A Twilight Struggle: American Power and Nicaragua*, The Free Press, 1996 p. 588.
67 *New-York Time*, 21 March 1988.
68 Robert Kagan, p. 589.
69 *The Washington Post*, 19 March 1988.
70 Robert Kagan, p. 591.

Chapter 8

1 Edme Dominguez Reyes, p. 113.
2 Stephen Kinzer, p. 305.
3 Laura M. Zaremba, p. 42.
4 Donald Castillo Rivas, p. 97.
5 Stephen Kinzer, pp. 373-374.
6 Luis Moreno, p. 203.
7 Gilles Bataillon, 'Contras et reContras nicaraguayens', p. 14.
8 *El Pais*, 4 May 1988.
9 Morales Carazo, 1989, p. 138.
10 Gilles Bataillon, ' Contraset reContras nicaraguayens', p. 14.
11 Thimothy C. Brown, *The Real Contra War*, p. 171.
12 Alain Rouquié, 1991, p. 211.
13 Luis Moreno, p. 205.
14 Wassim Draghir, p. 95.
15 Buvollen, 1989, p. 330.
16 Kinzer, p. 387.
17 Timothy C. Brown, *The Real Contra War*, p. 173.
18 Alain Rouquié, p. 225.
19 Laura M. Zaremba, p. 56.
20 Alain Rouquié, p. 246.
21 Timothy C. Brown, *The Real Contra War*, p. 175.
22 Francisco Barbosa Miranda, p. 57.
23 Randy Pestana and Brian Latell, *Nicaraguan Military Culture* (Florida International University, 2017), pp. 20-22.
24 Timothy C. Brown, *The Real Contra War*, p. 177. Comandancia General del Ejército de Nicaragua, p. 82.
25 Thimothy C. Brown, *The Real Contra War*, p. 183.
26 Randy Pestana and Brian Latell, p. 26.
27 *Le Monde*, 21 mars 2019.
28 Juan Avilés Farré, p. 306-308.
29 Krujit, p. 69.
30 Ibid, p. 74.
31 *NYT*, 20 February 1986.

ACKNOWLEDGEMENTS

This book would not have been possible without the assistance and support of an enthusiastic team who provided the author with valuable information and photos. I would like to thank them all warmly, especially Tom Cooper and Albert Grandolini. I would also like to thank the team of Helion & Company for their professionalism and the quality of their work. I dedicate this book to my parents for everything they have done for me.

AUTHOR

David François, from France, earned his PhD in Contemporary History at the University of Burgundy and specialised in studying militant communism, its military history and relationship between politics and violence in contemporary history. In 2009, he co-authored the *Guide des archives de l'Internationale communiste* published by the French National Archives and the Maison des sciences de l'Homme in Dijon. He is regularly contributing articles for various French military history magazines and is also a regular contributor to the French history website L'autre côté de la colline.